UNIT 6

Ideology: messages and values

Late in 1999, two men got together to discuss the creation of the world's biggest media corporation. Gerald Levin of Time-Warner said of his meeting with Steve Case of AOL:

> We had dinner, spent the entire time talking about values, world views and ideas and that's when it became clear to me that perhaps we should try and do it.
> (Quoted in Casey 2001)

A deal worth billions of dollars and affecting the whole of the world's media business, was sealed, partly at least, on the basis of a shared 'view of the world'. These men recognised that shared values and ideas about the world were as important to them as the economics of their business. Most people find it easier to get on with (or at least live and work closely with) others whose ideas and values they share, and peaceful social interaction is largely based on people sharing or accommodating each other's values and ideas about the world.

Media theory

One attribute of media texts is that they express and circulate 'ideas and values'. Examination specifications refer to media theory and the circulation of ideas under such headings as 'messages and values', ideology, hegemony and discourse. In this unit we look at these concepts and examine how an understanding of them helps us understand how films work with audiences. A Hollywood producer once denounced the idea of 'message pictures', saying that if he wanted to send the audience a message, he'd use a telegram. But Hollywood films – and all films at one level or another – deal in 'messages and values', though they are not necessarily obvious, or even consciously intended. If ideology operates as a process of naturalising certain ideas so that they appear as 'common sense', we need to develop strategies to expose its working.

We tend to take for granted many values in society as 'natural' and 'common sense'. How do you think your life will work out? Will you get married and become a parent? Many teenagers asked that question will probably answer 'Yes', because it seems like the 'natural' thing to do. But is it? The divorce rate is increasing, more people are cohabiting and the birth rate is at a historic low. If you decide not to get married, to get divorced or not to have children are you acting 'unnaturally'? Where does the idea that getting married is 'natural' come from? Is this idea changing to reflect changing reality or has it survived for some reason despite changes in society?

Two hundred years ago people married primarily for economic reasons. Now the prospect of marriage is linked to romance and we assume that the 'happy ending' to a romance will be a wedding. Yet, while marriage still has a high status, our ideas about marriage have to be seen next to our willingness to get divorced or to 'co-habit'. While some decisions we make are based on 'economics', others are influenced by our values and our ideas about the world.

Ideology

Ideology is concerned with ideas and values and how they evolve as a way of explaining the world around us. As people grow up they learn about the world through a variety of experiences – home, school, religious teachings, social events and, of course, access to media representations.

Marxism

In relation to ideology Media Studies is broadly influenced by the ideas of Karl Marx (1818-83). Marx wrote extensively about ideology in the mid-nineteenth century. Because his ideas became the basis for much political action in the twentieth century, the word 'ideology' has become something of a political football – nevertheless it is still a useful critical tool. For Marx, the process of learning about the world produced a 'false consciousness' – the ideas fitted together in such a way that they masked the reality of the individual's position in the world. Why, he wondered, did the mass of people put up with poverty and misery when their rulers enjoyed wealth and fulfilment?

itp
publications

bfi

According to Marx, throughout history the poor had been kept in their place by force of arms and by religious teachings that supported a strictly hierarchical society with land-owning aristocrats at the top and landless peasants at the bottom. Marx noted that under the new system of capitalism, the industrial workers were kept in their place not only by force of arms but also by an 'ideology' that evolved under capitalism, incorporating and modifying some traditional beliefs. For instance, selective reading of biblical sources promoted capitalist enterprise and ignored the more community-based ideals of much Christian teaching. Ideas about equality and inequality also evolved. Whereas in pre-capitalist society social inequality tended to be seen as being ordained by God, in capitalist society economic inequality tended to be justified in terms of how hardworking and enterprising a person might be. People were poor, capitalists believed, because they were lazy not because they were socially disadvantaged. Overall the capitalists succeeded in convincing most of the population that 'private profit was good' for society as a whole.

Marx set out a view of human history conceived as a struggle to control the means of producing wealth, primarily waged at the 'political' and 'economic' level. But his work on ideology also suggested another type of struggle at the level of the 'ideological' – a struggle to defend or challenge the dominant ideas in society. This can be explored by looking at what has happened to the idea of 'the family' over the last two hundred years.

Family values

In 1800, families did not consist only of parents and their offspring, but of a much wider group of relations and 'hangers on' who lived together. In poor families everybody worked – on the land or in cottage industries. In most rich families, men managed their estates and women lived a life of leisure in households where the domestic work was carried out by servants (many of whom were denied a family life).

Economic and political developments over the next century and a half demanded huge changes in family and community life. As the factory system developed under the industrial revolution the old social structures broke down. The collapse of the traditional economy and demands for labour in industrial centres forced families to move to find work, breaking up communities and causing social instability. Ideas about family life had to change to accommodate these changes, but also to provide a basis for social stability. The 'nuclear' family developed as a more mobile economic unit which enabled people to maintain close relationships even if they had to move away from their communities. Ideologically it also helped maintain social stability, partly at least because it gave people a close social group to identify with, a 'haven in a heartless world'. The family continued to change over the twentieth century, but the **idea** of the family that was developed during the nineteenth century – a mother, a father and their immediate offspring, where the father works and the mother looks after the family – has remained strongly influential.

The family on screen

The depiction of the typical American (and British) family in mainstream cinema has tended to reflect the nuclear family – both in endorsing and satirising it. The 'ideal' household has often been characterised as mum and dad and '2.4' children, the statistical average for many years. This family is represented in countless Hollywood 'family melodramas' and comedies, and in television comedies.

Pleasantville (US 1998) is a 'teen comedy' that gently satirises 1950s television family ideologies using the fantasy device of sending a pair of 1990s teenagers back to the 1950s and imprisoning them in the weird world of the television sitcom. What they discover is a world where mothers stay at home in their neat suburban homes baking pies while fathers go to work, returning home at the same time every day to proclaim 'Honey, I'm home!'. This phrase became the industry term for programmes in which all the stories were trivial and nothing 'bad' ever happened. We can laugh at this now, especially when we are surrounded by soap operas in which every kind of family is represented, yet the fifties idea of the 'ideal family' lives on in many ways and still has an influence on both representations and 'real world' policy decisions. In *Pleasantville*, the 1990s teenagers are from a single parent household (as in *Clueless* (1995) and many other modern teen comedies). This allows the film to both compare the 'cosiness' of the 1950s with the uncertainty of the 1990s, and find social benefits in aspects of life in the 1950s.

Once the ideal family has become the norm as a representation, it follows that any other kind of family, or any other kind of community or household in which people live together, is seen as at best different and at worst deviant. So family melodramas in the 1950s often dealt with the threat to the family posed by adultery or the impossibility of family life for single parents. Films and television dramas about the problems of living outside the ideal family served to reinforce the common sense idea that a nuclear family was essential to a happy and fulfilling life.

Any attempt to present a film in a realist style is likely to support the dominant ideology. Transparent realist and naturalist films of Hollywood tend to suggest that 'this is the way that the world is'. In order to break through the 'false consciousness' of the way in which we normally see the world, we must question the depiction of the world 'as is' and seek to understand why it is that way.

Exercise

- Conduct a simple 'content analysis' to find out how families are represented in the media.

- Log all the references to families in a range of media texts: television advertisements during an evening's viewing; TV soaps and sit-coms over a week; collecting newspapers and magazines and looking at both advertisements and news stories.

    - What kinds of families are represented?

    - Sort the different representations into those which are 'celebrated' and those which are in some way 'deviant'? (If a representation is an advertisement, think about what is being advertised and what approach is taken – are 'non-nuclear' families or households presented with humour, as 'odd', or with concern, as needing something special?)

    - Try to determine what kinds of narratives are associated with the representations of families. Do any patterns emerge?

Here are a couple of examples of the kind of analysis you might do:

Popstars

The 2000 docusoap about the creation of the band Hear'Say offered a fascinating insight into the way in which the press quickly 'typed' the band members. Kim was picked out as a single parent, something she had initially kept secret, and this became not only a distinguishing feature, but also a way of emphasising her 'difference' and suggesting narratives about her – how would it affect her future career, what potential stories will develop?

Erin Brockovich

In the opening section of *Erin Brockovich*, when Erin is being cross-examined in court in her claim for damages, the defendant's counsel asks her a question and she reveals that she has not one, but two ex-husbands. She is now a single woman with three small children and two divorces behind her. She looks at the jury in defiance. They look apprehensive and Erin loses her temper. The inference is clear – Erin is either foolish or wilful, but she isn't to be trusted. The court leaps to the conclusion that she married without enough thought and that losing her temper is a typical character flaw. Ideology rather than legal evidence wins the court case and the 'nice' middle-class doctor is believed (when we know he was responsible for the accident).

Other ways of thinking about ideology – hegemony and discourse

The original conception of ideology was that it was concerned with social attitudes based firmly upon economic differences – for Marx, ideology was a function of the control over the means of production. The dominant ideology was that of the ruling industrial class and its effect was to 'naturalise' the domination of the working class by the industrialists. In the twentieth century the ideological came to be seen as important in its own right and not simply 'determined' by economics. Philosophers and political thinkers developed alternative ways of thinking about ideology, specifically 'hegemony' and 'discourse'.

Hegemony

This term derives from political history and refers to the power of one country over several others. In Media Studies the term is associated with the Italian theorist and political activist, Antonio Gramsci (1891-1937). He emphasised that the control of society by one group or one set of political ideas was not necessarily achieved by force or control of arms, but by persuasion and 'consent' – the basis for democracy. The rulers manage to convince the mass of the population that they are 'better off' accepting current government policies. Maintaining hegemonic control is thus a process of constantly reinforcing the message and developing the argument.

The concept of hegemony allows for substantial changes in ideas over time, even though the same groups remain in power. These groups constantly adjust their own ideas and find new ways to gain the consent of those they dominate. Hegemony is a useful concept because it suggests that people can try to understand how the dominant ideas remain dominant – Gramsci was a great supporter of improvements in education.

It could be argued that 'hegemonic power' is exerted by the Hollywood studios through their overseas trade organisation, the MPAA (Motion Pictures Association of America). In one sense this is hegemony in the traditional 'political history' definition: the studios 'occupy' most countries by owning cinemas and distributors, usually in partnership with local companies. They can ensure that their films get shown. But the studios also work in the Gramscian sense of an hegemonic power, 'persuading' us that their films are the best and that we have a right to see them. This operates at government level with the powerful MPAA lobby arguing for a 'free market' in films in Europe and at the popular level with the appearance of Hollywood stars at film festivals and on chat shows in a 'charm offensive'. Politicians and industry professionals may be well aware of the economic power that the MPAA wields but audiences across the world are always willing to accept 'glamorous' and exciting American films. Nobody forces audiences to watch American films, but in reality they have little choice since Hollywood dominates the film industry.

Discourse

The French theorist Michel Foucault (1926-84) is credited with introducing ideas about 'discourse' into cultural theory. Foucault was interested in power relationships and the ways in which language can be used to wield power. He challenged the traditional view of language as neutral, as simply describing reality, and argued that language creates meaning by the way in which it is used.

Discourse can be thought of as an arena in which certain words are used. In the arena, it is rarely a fair fight – some of the gladiators are better at using and manipulating words. It is a struggle at the level of the ideological, a struggle with words rather than weapons, but a 'real' struggle nonetheless.

The way words are used to describe people offers a good example of how 'discourse' works. What does it mean if someone calls anyone over the age of 18 a 'girl' or a 'boy'? 'Girl' as a description of a woman implies perhaps that they have not yet grown up, that they are not to be treated as adults – not to be given responsibility or 'grown-up' tasks. Does the male manager, who refers to his female staff as the 'girls', take them seriously? It suggests that there is a power relationship involved here, in contrast to the way women themselves may use 'girls' as a title in a phrase like 'a girls' night out'. Women may use the term themselves when they want to have fun and to 'let themselves go', but this is only possible because they have reclaimed the word so it becomes a code hinting at a sense of solidarity against the men who treat them as 'girls'. Similarly in African-American culture, the use of the word 'nigger' between two black men gains its power by usurping the racist term used by whites. 'Gay' used to be a derogatory term to describe homosexual men, but has now been adopted as an acceptable and celebratory label.

Exercise

- Think about the use of the term 'boy' to describe adult males.

    - How many different ways can it be used?

    - What kinds of power relationships are involved?

('Boy' was used as a racist term in America before the Civil Rights movement of the 1960s. One of the ways in which slaver owners maintained control was to type slaves as 'child-like' and unable to govern themselves.)

Applied to films, the concept of discourse can be used with any form of meaning production – visual images and sound effects, as well as spoken language. A discourse analysis would look for sets of related images in a film, all dealing with the same issue. There could be several discourses operating in the text at the same time, so in a film like *Terminator* (US 1984) there is a discourse about gender (the transformation of Sarah Connor from fluffy waitress to warrior battling the very 'male' cyborg) and about technology and its impact on society.

Discourse analysis is useful because it allows readers to get beneath the surface of the text and to discover how ideas are being represented systematically. We can note instances of images that seem to belong to a specific discourse and analyse the struggle over ideas represented by competing discourses. This analysis may reveal aspects of the film's ideology that are not obvious when we first watch a film.

Research Exercise

- What are the discourses operating in *Erin Brockovich* or *The Insider*?

References

Gill Branston and Roy Stafford (1999) *The Media Student's Book*, Routledge, Chapter 12

John Casey (2001), Gerald Levin Interview, Guardian 10 March

TEACHERS' NOTES

Representation: the key questions

Most teachers will approach Key Concepts in an integrated way and no assumptions are made here about how or when the concept of representation will be introduced. It is assumed that most courses will begin with an introductory analysis of a media text and an attempt to outline the Key Concepts. The materials in the pack are organised around five key questions which make up the field of study.

• What sense of the world is this film making? (What kind of world does the film construct?)

• What does it claim is typical of the world? (How are familiar 'types' used in the film as a form of shorthand to represent people?)

• Who is really speaking? (Who is in control of the representations in the film – whose values and ideas are expressed in the film?)

• For whom? (Will different audiences make different readings of the film?)

• What does it represent for us and why? (To what extent are the representations in the film part of the struggle in the 'real world' to either maintain or change the power relationships between groups of people or sets of ideas and values? What is the political role of representations?)

[Based on Richard Dyer (1985) 'Taking popular television seriously' in Philip Drummond and David Lusted (eds) *Television and Schooling*, bfi.]

These questions indicate the complexity of any analysis of representation. We explore them in relation to three films *Erin Brockovich, Mildred Pierce* and *The Insider*. This will enable a comparison of related representations both across time (*Mildred Pierce* to *Erin Brockovich*) and across genre.

Unit 1 introduces the five key questions while Units 2-6 explore each question in turn. The two Case Studies offer the chance of developing students' understanding of representation through making comparisons between *Erin Brockovich, Mildred Pierce* and *The Insider* (extracts from these films can be used if there is not time to include complete screenings – specific extracts are suggested Case Studies 1 and 2).

In Case Study 1 we apply the five key questions to *Erin Brockovich* and compare this film with *The Insider*, addressing the different approaches to realism and the discourse of social class. (This Case Study also supports students undertaking the OCR module on American Cinema and Social Class: see the separate note on this.)

Case Study 2 focuses on *Mildred Pierce* and *Erin Brockovich* in the context of the woman's picture and explores the treatment of gender issues in both films and in *The Insider*.

Finally, the three short studies extend the range of film examples to include *Lola rennt (Run Lola Run), La Haine* and *The Piano*. These three films have been used extensively with AS and A Level students and have generated strong involvement with representational issues. By moving outside Hollywood to consider European and New Zealand representations they offer an alternative mode of study and the potential to widen student experience. Each film has been chosen to enable study of specific representational issues which can be related back to the units. Students can extend their exploration of the issues of representations through studying these films. Alternatively, one of the three films in the Short Studies could become a major focus of classroom work with less attention paid to *Erin Brockovich*. The films in the Short Studies are more challenging, but they are accessible and will present students with more 'meaty' representation issues.

References are included with each unit and a full Bibliography and Filmography is supplied in this pack.

Knowledge of 'film language'

If students are to produce high quality writing about representation in film, it is important that they are well practised in close analysis of specific film sequences. This means that they must be familiar with specialist terminology and the range of concepts associated with camerawork, lighting, production design, sound and editing. There is not space in this pack to introduce film language as such but the Case Studies include good examples of close reading supporting study of representation issues. Working through these examples should provide good practice for students and indicate the types of textual evidence that might appear in examination answers. (Also see 'An Introduction to Film Language', an Interactive CD-ROM published by *bfi* Education.)

Terminology and student reading

The Units have been designed as student notes and should be accessible to both AS and A2 students. The materials included in the pack have been used in public events with students (ie as the basis for presentations and discussions) and the level has been found to be appropriate. However in AS classes, in particular, there is a wide range of reading ability and teachers may wish to support students by working through some sections in more detail and adding their own gloss.

The four examination and coursework specifications addressed here sometimes use different theoretical terms to describe the same concept. The only time this creates a potential problem is in Unit 6. The OCR specification refers to 'messages and values' whereas both AQA and WJEC use the term 'ideology'. Since the latter is more clearly defined in Media Studies literature, it has been used here.

Acquiring film and related materials

For the work on film analysis suggested in the pack, you will need a video copy of *Erin Brockovich, Mildred Pierce* and *The Insider*. If DVD facilities are available, the DVD copies of *Erin Brockovich* and *The Insider* are highly recommended as they both come with extra material which will support a representation study. It is also important to use the widescreen (1:2.35) version of *The Insider* in order to fully appreciate the compositions featuring the relationship between Jeffrey Wigand and Lowell Bergman and also Michael Mann's general approach to *mise en scène*. (It is always important to use films in their correct aspect ratio if this is possible.)

Getting started

Unit 1 – Representation – an introduction

Objectives: Students should

1. be able to define 'representation';

2. know the five key questions that will enable them to explore issues of representation.

Many students find it easiest to engage with conceptual work after working through a text. The best starting point for this pack is a screening of *Erin Brockovich* and a general discussion about how to read a film. A useful question to start with is:

How should we approach *Erin Brockovich*? As:

• a Julia Roberts film?

• a Steven Soderbergh film?

• a genre picture?

• a true story?

• a film about pollution?

This discussion will raise the general question of representation – what is the film trying to say about the world, about Erin Brockovich herself or about the specific case of environmental damage?

From here, it is possible to outline the key questions in Unit 1. These key questions are elaborated on in Units 2-6 which you can take in any order. Alternatively, you could use Case Study 1, which draws on each of the key questions in turn, as the focus of your course, using the additional information as required from each of the units.

Unit 2 – Realism

Objectives: Students should

1. understand the concept of realism and that there are many different ways of representing the world in film;

2. learn that the appearance of reality is constructed.

A useful way of starting work on realism is to study a range of short extracts from films mentioned in the pack, concentrating on the characters moving in their environment. The two extracts mentioned in the first exercise in Case Study 1 include short scenes in which we see Erin Brockovich get into her car only to head straight into an accident and Lowell Bergman meet Jeffrey Wigand in a Louisville hotel. This offers a contrast between 'naturalistic/observational' and 'expressionistic' styles. A scene from *The Piano* showing the characters moving through the 'expressionist' forest and from *La Haine* showing the youths on the estate could be used to reinforce the distinction. The start of the first run of Lola in *Lola rennt* includes an animation sequence, which works to suggest the metaphor of a computer game.

Ask students to group or contrast the extracts according to these questions:

• Are the characters being presented to us as ordinary people or as larger than life characters?

• Is the location being presented 'as is' in the world we know or as a theatrical set in which we expect high drama?

• Is the director appealing to our knowledge of the world we live in or to our knowledge of other films?

This should be relatively straightforward with *Erin/La Haine* on one side and *The Insider/The Piano* on the other. Lola is interesting because she is both an animated hero and an ordinary young woman. A full coverage of the ideas in the unit will mean looking at an extract from an avowedly social realist film such as Ken Loach's *Raining Stones* and at a film that plays with ideas of realism such as *The Blair Witch Project*.

It is useful if students are aware of the concept of 'anti-realism' (Category 4) but it may be difficult to find contemporary examples. The 'anti-realist' idea can be illustrated by pointing to any cinematic device that breaks 'realist' conventions. This includes characters talking directly to the camera and surrealist jokes that disrupt the transparency of the image. These sometimes appear in mainstream comedies such as *Blazing Saddles* (US 1973), the spoof western in which a chase around the desert reveals the studio orchestra playing the music behind a large rock. In *A Selfmade Hero* (France 1996) the story is punctuated by music from an on-screen string quartet. This film can be used to discuss realism and anti-realism.

The units in this pack make up an integrated scheme of work. In Unit 6 realism is critiqued as a conservative aesthetic that doesn't challenge how ideas about the world are constructed and presented. This is a point that may be easiest to make using the traditional 'form and content' distinction. 'Social realist' films in particular are quite likely to be progressive in content, focusing attention on important social issues, but they are conservative in formal terms. Films that use fantasy and expressionism may deal only with seemingly escapist material but their formal experimentation can move audiences to think differently and therefore subvert conventional behaviour.

Unit 3 – Analysing the typical

Objectives: Students should understand that

1. films use 'types' as a central reference point for their construction of character;

2. characters in films can be represented on a continuum between 'typical' or 'individual' (or novelistic) depending on the type of film and their role in it.

This unit explores how people are characterised in film, with some comparison with the novel. You could introduce this unit by making a list of well-known characters from films on the board and asking students to discuss to what extent they are representing types of people or unique individuals.

Exercise: Deconstructing types

In the films they select for this exercise, students may use their own knowledge and experience to draw out the cultural references in relation to types. However, an example of this sort of deconstruction can be carried out in relation to *O Brother, Where Art Thou*?. The points you could draw out include:

• The Ulysses reference:

George Clooney plays the role of Ulysses McGill. The film is based on an amalgam of Homer's *Odyssey* and a 1930s/40s 'screwball comedy', *Sullivan's Travels*, directed by Preston Sturges. What do students know about Ulysses? Ulysses is the archetypal 'leader of a group of adventurers' from Greek legends and also the generic comic 'screwball character' of the man who is clever but not sensible.

• Stereotyping the 'Deep South':

All the roles in the film, including Ulysses McGill, derive something from the stereotypes associated with the 'Deep South', especially during the 1930s – rural 'dumb hicks', lacking sophistication, ill-educated, credulous and addicted to hillbilly music.

• The star:

Clooney himself brings a star image associated with smooth sophistication that can be reversed in this role. The 1930s setting also allows him to 'play' with the idea of becoming a modern day Clark Gable, leading star of studio era Hollywood, complete with pencil moustache.

Unit 4 – Whose voice?

Objectives: Students should understand that

1. films are constructed by creative teams;

2. the ideas and values 'spoken' in the film are not necessarily those of the people the film purports to represent.

A useful way into this unit is to refer to the screening of *Erin Brockovich* and/or *The Insider* or any other film students have recently watched. Ask them whose 'view' is being most strongly expressed through the film. Is the director trying to get across a particular message? Does the star have any influence over what is being said? Who else might be influential in the construction of the film? How might the 'message' or 'standpoint' of the film be influenced by its backers?

The discussion of 'voice' needs to be dealt with quite subtly both because the answer to 'whose voice?' is not entirely straightforward, and because most films are made by people who themselves have probably never experienced what the characters in the film are going through. Instead they are collectively, through their individual contributions to the whole project, trying to convey something about the characters and what they represent. The producer and director probably have the strongest influence over what is conveyed through the film, but the star and other members of the production team may also have some input in terms of their own interpretations of what the film is about. The point to emphasise is that films don't simply reflect society. Perhaps 'refract' might be a better metaphor. Films exist within society, they interact with events and changing attitudes.

Unit 5 – Ideas about audience

Objectives: Students should understand that audiences

1. may interpret representations in different ways according to their own cultural experiences;

2. influence the construction of representations through their expectations of star performances and the decisions they make about what kinds of films to watch.

This unit refers to the recent increase in the opportunities for audiences to discuss the films they see and to develop their interest in particular stars and films. This is apparent in the growth of internet sites with 'user comments' on films as well as 'fan sites' and 'preview sites' (ie speculation about future films). Access to the Internet Movie Database, Amazon etc. will enable students to get a sense of different audience responses around the world, and also to observe how star personae are being developed.

The unit includes a short questionnaire designed to aid students in reflecting on their own responses to films and some of the possible reasons why they might 'read' films in particular ways. It focuses specifically on age and gender. The conclusions they draw from the results of a survey can be compared with conclusions drawn from analysing 'user comments' on the internet.

Unit 6 – Ideology

Objectives: Students should understand that

1. ideology plays an important role in the construction of representations;

2. there are different ways of thinking about ideology including discourse theory and the theory of hegemony.

The ideas and the student exercises in Unit 6 are important for students at all levels, but AS teachers may wish to use this Unit selectively, perhaps re-introducing it at A2. This is quite a complex unit, however, don't be afraid to have a go with it, though you may need to help some students 'unpick' it. You could start by asking the students whether they can identify a particular world view being presented in any of the films you have chosen to focus on. Are *Erin Brockovich* or *The Insider* promoting or challenging any particular interests? Are they promoting or challenging any particular view of, or implying any judgements about the role of, women or men in society? Are they setting up any 'ideal' about how individuals should behave?

Case Study 1

This can be used as a reference point through out the study of representation or given to students to help them consolidate their learning. An extra note is provided on the understanding of social class in America.

Exercise – representing real events

In this exercise students are asked to compare how reality is reconstructed in the two films. Although both films fit broadly into the concept of 'Hollywood realism' and 'transparency', *Erin* is at one 'pole', moving towards social realism/naturalism, and *The Insider* is at the opposite pole, moving towards an expressionist style (see Unit 2 for definitions). We could show differences like this:

Erin

Camera is a detached observer

More long shots

'Open', non-threatening *mise en scène*

'Natural' light

Location unremarkable

The Insider

Camera is more like a spy, an investigator, hand-held 'wobble' suggests uncertainty

More close-ups

Framings 'cut-off' or blocked by doors, windows, furniture etc.

'Disturbing' *mise en scène*

Lighting is more 'low-key' with expressionist shadows

Location emphasises windows, corridors, doors

The visual style in this sequence offers clues about genre. The expressionist style of *The Insider* suggests the thriller and especially the conspiracy or 'paranoia thriller' – the sense that the characters are constantly under surveillance. This is confirmed by Russell Crowe's edgy performance.

Case Study 2

This case study explores gender representation in relation to film genres. Assigning a film to specific genre is not necessarily straightforward and in itself may not be particularly illuminating. However, it is possible to recognise a mix of generic references and analyse how these help construct representations. The historical evolution of how women are represented in society is explored in relation to *Erin Brockovich* and *Mildred Pierce* – two films made nearly 50 years apart. The representation of the male hero is explored in relation to *The Insider*, which could lead to a further exploration for interested students of how the representation of men has changed in the last 50 years.

Short studies

The three films analysed here provide additional material for the study of representation. You may prefer either to give students a copy of each study separately after watching the relevant film, or to give them all to the students and ask them to choose one of the films to explore in more detail as an individual study.

Further suggestions for work on specific films and combinations of films are given under the filmography.

CONTENTS & OBJECTIVES

Objectives

Representation is one of the Key Concepts for Film and Media Studies at AS and A2. Knowledge and understanding about representation issues are assessed at both levels across a range of modules and students are also expected to be aware of representation issues in their practical production work. The materials in the pack will be useful in addressing a wide range of issues, but the main focus is on gender representation with some coverage of class and ethnicity.

This pack focuses on representations in fiction films, using examples drawn from Hollywood and European Cinema. The same ideas and approaches explored here can be applied to non-fiction films as well as television programmes. Film has been chosen as the focus of the pack, both because of its popularity with students and also because specific film titles are available on video (VHS and DVD). All the main titles discussed in the pack are available at the time of writing and because of their general high profile, are likely to remain so for some time to come.

The main aims of this pack are:
- to encourage students towards conceptual understanding, so that they are able to distance themselves from the texts being studied and engage in a critical analysis of how representations are constructed

- to support students in writing about representation issues and particularly in using appropriate evidence drawn from close textual analysis

Specification references

- AQA: AS/1 Reading the Media, AS/2 Textual Topic Film and Broadcast Fiction, A2/4 Texts and Contexts in the Media A2/5 Possible topic for Independent Study

- OCR: AS/1 Textual Analysis: Section B Option – American Cinema and Social Class, A2/5: Women and Film Option, A2/6 Media Issues and Debates (Film option)

- WJEC: AS2 Media Representations and Reception, A2 Unit 4 Investigating Media Texts

- WJEC Film Studies: Useful in introducing the key concept and aspects of work across the course including stars and performance (Unit 6)

© British Film Institute

itp
publications

bfi

Films illustrated in the strip:
Lola rennt (Run Lola Run) (1998 X Film Creative Pool) Erin Brockovich (2000 Columbia Pictures)

UNIT 1

Representation – an introduction

It is generally recognised that all media texts are 'constructed', that is put together by creative and technical teams who follow standard procedures for selecting, compiling and editing material. Documentaries and news programmes on television are just as 'constructed' as fiction films made for the cinema.

Defining 'representation'

According to one writer (Dyer, 1985) representation can be looked at in the following ways:

- As re-presentation: presenting reality over again to us. Reality is mediated through forms of representation available in the culture.

- As 'being representative of' in the sense of being 'typical'. This, of course, raises the question of what is 'typical'.

- In the sense of speaking for and on behalf of somebody or a group.

- In recognising the existence of audience responses, with different audiences responding to different kinds of representation.

In this introductory unit on representation we will briefly look at how film developed as a representational medium and identify the main questions we need to explore in order to understand how 'representation' works in film.

The development of film as a representational medium

Photographic realism

Cinema inherited the idea of photographic realism. Photography is a medium that works by 'capturing' images as gradations of light and shade on a light sensitive emulsion. The new medium, developed in the first half of the nineteenth century, could have been used primarily to create abstract images composed of shapes, colours and textures (a modern version of this might be the 'light shows' in clubs and bars). But it became apparent very quickly that the popularity of photography derived from its ability to record images of people, places and objects – a form of 'mechanical reproduction'. By the late nineteenth century it had become common practice to record images of big public events as well as the 'personal' milestones of life such as childhood, marriage etc.

The beginnings of cinema

As well as photographic realism, cinema also drew on other forms of art and entertainment such as theatre, music hall and dance. In the twentieth century it added sound and colour – expanding the range of representational devices. Cinema could have developed in many ways, but the dominant form became a narrative cinema, telling stories over ninety minutes or so and using 'iconic' images – 'resemblances' of images in the real world. A film is essentially a series of events recorded by the camera. In examining the processes of representation we will focus, in part, on the technology and techniques of cinema and the way we 'read' cinematic images by recognising certain techniques and drawing meaning from them.

Cinema and cultural context

Popular cinema is based upon a common understanding of the social world. Over the last 100 years and more of filmmaking, a language or grammar of images and sounds has evolved that allows filmmakers to represent this world. Audiences – exposed to film and television, often from an early age – learn this language quickly and the cultural knowledge that we require to understand popular cinema is not something we usually call upon consciously. It has been 'naturalised' so that the process of constructing meaning through creating representations, as undertaken by filmmakers, has become invisible.

itp publications

bfi

Audiences

The construction of representations may have been rendered invisible (or to put it another way, the constructional devices have become transparent – we see through them to the constructed meaning), but this doesn't mean that audiences just lie back and let films simply roll over them. In any audience there will be individuals or groups of individuals who read an image or a sequence in a film in different ways. Filmmakers cannot rigidly fix a representation and demand that their audiences understand the film in a certain way. Representations can be reinterpreted and made to have different meanings by people watching the film – though it could be argued that the viewer's first task is to try to understand what the filmmakers are trying to represent.

Five key questions

Here are five key questions that can be used in exploring the term 'representation' and reflect the complexity of any analysis of representation (adapted from Richard Dyer, 1985):

• What sense of the world is this film making? (What kind of world does the film construct?)

• What does it claim is typical of the world? (How are familiar 'types' used in the film as a form of shorthand to represent people?)

• Who is really speaking? (Who is in control of the representations in the film – whose values and ideas are expressed in the film?)

• For whom? (Will different audiences make different readings of the film?)

• What does it represent for us and why? (Does 'representation' have a political role in, for example, maintaining power relations?)

The critical task – a note to students

A typical Media Studies exam or coursework assessment will require analysis of specific representations in a selected media text. Where it is possible to select a film, you will usually write about a particular sequence, often the beginning or ending of a film or a pivotal sequence in the middle of the film. Critical work will involve thinking about the techniques used by filmmakers, the relationship between the fictional world and the real world – the cultural context – and the importance of the audience. The important points to bear in mind in answering questions on representation in films are:

• You should provide 'evidence' for any assertion you make: you need to demonstrate your ability to 'read' sequences in terms of their use of film language. Representations are constructed though camerawork, sound and editing and you should write about images in these terms.

• All your work on the Key Concepts of narrative, genre, audience and institution should be integrated: you may need to refer to them in your response to questions about representation.

References

Richard Dyer (1985) 'Taking popular television seriously' in Philip Drummond and David Lusted (eds) *Television and Schooling, bfi*

UNIT 2

Realism

One of the main reasons why we enjoy films is because they appear to represent the 'real world', a world that is both familiar and new to us – or they play with the idea of what is 'real'. However, the real can't simply be 'captured' by the camera or the microphone and put on screen. What appears on screen will always be the result of choices and selection.

The main points we want to explore in this unit are:

• There are many different ways of representing the real world on a cinema screen.

• The 'effect' of realism can only be created through considerable 'artifice' – realism only emerges through construction.

There are few words that can carry as many different meanings as the trio of 'real', 'realist' and 'realism'. In this unit we do not want to get mired in a complicated philosophical discussion about what is 'real' but we do want to understand how films represent the 'real world' – the world we negotiate every day.

Representing the real

We can distinguish five broad categories of representations of the world:

1. Films which are 'transparent' in presenting events – the dominant style of Hollywood cinema that does not draw attention to itself. Camerawork, sound and editing are designed to facilitate easy access to the story and the events unfold in a logical manner. The fictional world is recognisable, but the people and the events are usually 'larger than life' (more beautiful, more talented, events are more exciting etc) and we must suspend our disbelief if the film is going to be enjoyable.

2. Films which present events drawn from everyday social life and which adopt a camera, sound and editing style that draws attention to the 'authenticity' of the events (ie we would experience them like this in the 'real world'). These might be described as '**social realist**', but note that there are several different realist styles and therefore several different cinematic 'realisms'.

3. Films which are clearly '**fantastic**' – events are depicted that could not, or at least are very unlikely to happen in 'real' life. The camerawork, sound and editing may be used more 'expressionistically'. Despite the element of fantasy, these representations will still have something to say about the 'real world'. For example, audiences and critics are interested in the character of Ripley in the *Alien* series as well as what the film has to say about gender politics. The differences between the 'transparent' and the 'fantastic' type of film may be very slight. A comedy set in an office, like *What Women Want* (US 2001), is 'transparent', but *Being John Malkovich* (US 2000), in which characters physically gain access to the actor's brain, is a fantasy. On the other hand, a science fiction film, which presents events as logically based on scientific ideas, is likely to be 'transparent'.

4. Films which deny the possibility of a 'realist' representation and which therefore dispense with the usual conventions of (fiction) filmmaking. These films 'foreground' the process of making a film or 'constructing' a story – so that actors talk directly to camera, the camera is in shot, events are presented out of sequence etc. They might be described as '**anti-realist**'. However, although this approach is based on a denial that 'realism' is either possible or useful, this does not mean that it cannot comment on the 'real world'. Indeed filmmakers supporting this approach would argue that it is the only way to expose the reality that is usually obscured in mainstream films. This category is rare in contemporary cinema and almost unknown in Hollywood. It is largely a product of the so-called 'counter cinema' movement of the 1960s and 1970s. However, aspects of the approach surface occasionally (eg the re-organisation of the narrative in *Pulp Fiction* (US 1994)). A classic example of anti-realism comes in Jean Luc Godard's *Tout va bien* (France 1972) about a strike in a factory. The film begins by showing the two stars (Yves Montand and Jane Fonda) signing their contracts and accepting cheques for working on the film, while a voiceover addresses the audience. This technique emphasises the constructed-ness of the film.

5. Films which 'play' with the idea of 'realism'. Often identified as examples of contemporary '**postmodern**' culture, films like *The Blair Witch Project* (US 1999) or 'mockumentaries' like *This Is Spinal Tap* (US 1984) use realist techniques, but they are essentially concerned with commenting on other films rather than dealing directly with the 'real world'. This is a central feature of the idea of 'postmodernity' – that audiences make sense of a film, and derive pleasure from it, through their knowledge of other films, rather than their knowledge of the world. This category is a very loose definition, but it is important to recognise that the whole concept of 'realism in the cinema' has come into question and we need to emphasise the fluidity of definitions.

All forms of representing the 'real world' work with 'codes and conventions' of realism. Realism is not simply a 'slice of reality' but a set of conventions about how to represent reality. For instance, most films that deal with the historical past provide careful reproductions of clothing, hairstyles, architecture and furnishings because they can do this accurately and because audiences expect it. But no one can be sure how people spoke 500 years ago and audiences today probably wouldn't understand the accents anyway. So 'authentic speech' is not a realist convention and even if it was the film would use subtitles – another convention.

Social vs transparent realism

We need to distinguish between Hollywood's 'transparent realism' (Category 1) and 'social realism' (Category 2). It is perhaps easier to try and define 'social realism' first.

Social realism

This concept derives largely from the so-called 'neo-realist' movement in Italy in the 1940s. The essence of neo-realism was the idea that the story came out of the life on the street, or the village. As Roberto Rossellini put it 'the subject of the film is the world'. (Rossellini 1953). In other words, the filmmaker's aim is to put 'reality' on the screen, not to invent a story and use reality as the backdrop. Allied to this concentration on social issues as subject 'content' was an aesthetic or 'style' that included:

• shooting on authentic locations;

• using non-professional actors or actors with the correct class/region background for the characters;

• using long takes and an 'observational', documentary-type camera style;

• not using theme music or special effects.

In the 1940s the idea of location shooting went against the standard idea of 'creating' and controlling the representation of the 'real world' in the studio. The new approach was perhaps less radical in Britain where documentary filmmakers had already had a major impact on fiction filmmaking during the Second World War.

The neo-realist approach was taken up by new filmmakers in Asia, Africa and Latin America, partly because it was the least expensive approach to production, but also because of its focus on social issues. In Hollywood, the vogue for realism in the late 1940s was developed by leftwing writers and producers who began to explore social issues. This being Hollywood, many of these issues (such as anti-semitism in *Crossfire* (US 1947)), were worked into crime narratives, often filmed on the streets of New York. Something of the feel for New York streets developed in the late 1940s survives in contemporary television police series such as *NYPD Blue*.

The best-known modern exponents of social realism are probably British directors, Ken Loach and Mike Leigh. Although they approach production in distinct ways and their characters are constructed differently, both are concerned to offer films about 'ordinary lives' in recognisable locations. In Loach's case this has tended to be the Britain of council housing estates in London (*Ladybird, Ladybird*), Manchester (*Raining Stones*) or Glasgow (*My Name is Joe*). Loach's films are often labelled as 'grim' or 'bleak' by unfriendly critics. However, the films offer both comedy and melodrama, though Loach does not add false 'glamour' or special effects. Audience pleasure is expected to derive from engagement with the characters and their predicaments, which are mundane and familiar (eg in *Raining Stones*, a family is thrown into crisis because an unemployed man is determined to buy his daughter a communion dress).

Representations in social realist films are concerned with a sense of location and the credibility of the characters. Loach's actors (and Leigh's) are drawn from a pool of working class talent with clear regional identities (including Robert Carlyle in *Riff Raff* and *Carla's Song*, Peter Mullan in *My Name is Joe*, and Ray Winstone in *Ladybird, Ladybird*).

Andrew Higson has suggested that one of the defining features of the British New Wave films of the 1960s (which were directly associated with social realism) was 'That Long Shot of Our Town from That Hill' (Higson 1984). The filmmakers confirmed the sense of authenticity by showing a cityscape with mills and foundries and the rows of workers' 'back-to-back' houses. The 1960s films also benefited from an influx of young acting talent with Northern working class roots (Albert Finney, Tom Courtenay etc) – many of the successful middle class film stars of the period could not play credible characters in these films. In Loach's films of the 1990s, a similar defining image of 'place' is the long shot showing the central characters, often in a battered transit van, driving through an estate of high-rise flats.

Ken Loach reflects on his approach to shooting in a realist style:

> I think you should feel subconsciously that the objects in the frame are balanced, but if you come out of a shot and say 'Ah, yes, isn't that a stunning frame?' then you've lost the point of it. It should seem just right, although in an implicit rather than predictable way. It shouldn't strike you as a self-consciously beautiful shot; that's showing off.

> I think you need to communicate the sense of landscape, but it's the landscape that is beautiful, not the shot. It's important that you link the audience to the landscape as unselfconsciously as you can.
> (Loach interviewed in Fuller, 1998)

Naturalism vs Expressionism

Naturalism

Naturalism derives from the theatre in the nineteenth century when actors stopped speaking and gesturing towards the audience and attempted to speak and act more naturally or realistically. Although early cinema used the stylised gestures of traditional theatre, modern cinema tends towards the naturalistic approach.

Naturalist acting is still a 'construct' – a style of acting. Some actors adopt the approach of trying to 'become' their character, finding ways to be 'absorbed' into someone else's personality, and therefore to represent it more realistically. (This is the basis of 'Method' acting popular from the 1950s through to the 1970s.)

Likewise, naturalistic camerawork attempts to depict the world 'as we see it'. It requires great skill to 'disguise' the construction (ie the movement of the camera and changing of the lens). This style is found in Hollywood 'transparent realist' films as well as 'social realist' films.

Naturalism is only one way of representing 'the real'. For instance, the hand-held camera and the wobbly 'subjective' shot is not part of naturalism because it represents the character's point of view, and is not an attempt to represent a general perspective on reality.

Exercise

Place the following films and TV programmes along a continuum from 'naturalist' to 'non-naturalist':

> ER, EastEnders, The Blair Witch Project, This Life, Ally McBeal, Sleepy Hollow, Erin Brockovich, My Name is Joe, The Sopranos, Casualty, Teachers

Overall, naturalism is opposed by 'expressionism'.

Expressionism

Expressionism is an art movement that emerged in the early twentieth century. In film the term 'expressionist' refers to a way of presenting an image so that the character's emotions are expressed through the depiction of the 'external world'. This style is also intended to evoke an emotional response in the audience. Lighting, camerawork, art direction and music can all be used 'expressionistically'.

In a genre such as horror, the disturbed mind of a character or the existence of secret thoughts can be expressed through shadows, angled compositions and distorted views.

Realist films will tend to avoid expressionism. It is important to note the difference between the shadows created by the use of natural light in a realist/naturalist film and the shadows intended to be seen expressionistically in a thriller (though it is, of course, possible to consciously mix the two in a 'realist thriller').

Exercise

• Identify some films you have watched that use a mixture of naturalism and expressionism.

Realism and the 'transparent' Hollywood film

The clearest difference between Hollywood and social realism is in the approach to the material. In broad terms, social realist filmmakers want to explore social issues, using individual stories as a focus for films set in specific locations. The purpose of social realism is to educate and inform (while being entertaining); the appeal to realism is perhaps to add weight to the argument. Hollywood generally does the opposite – presenting an exciting story about an individual with social issues as background. The purpose of a Hollywood film is to entertain and the realism should support that purpose by involving the audience in the story.

Two interesting films to compare in terms of realism are Spike Lee's *Do The Right Thing* (US 1989) and John Singleton's *Boyz 'N the Hood* (US 1991). Singleton tries to show Los Angeles 'as is', whereas Lee wants to make his own statement:

> … starting from a tangible reality (the film was actually shot on Stuyvesant Avenue between Quincy Street and Lexington Avenue), Spike Lee performs a series of manipulations that artfully transform a very real setting into a theatrical stage… He chooses an area of Brooklyn that symbolizes the black ghetto with its substandard housing and record-high number of welfare recipients. Yet Lee's black ghetto is not devastated by poverty, unemployment and drug abuse. If Lee's stylized Bed-Stuy is so different from the Los Angeles ghetto depicted by filmmaker John Singleton, it is because Lee's aesthetic concerns deliberately overshadow the depth and intensity of racial and economic exclusion.
> (Catherine Pouzoulet 1997)

Realism and emotion

One way in which Hollywood has embraced an idea of realism is in respect to emotion and the experience of cinema. Since the 1920s Hollywood has been at the forefront of technological developments designed to find ways of making the experience of sitting in a cinema seat more 'real' – closer to a situation in which the sounds and images on the screen overwhelm the audience. As the advertising for IMAX, the most spectacular form of cinema, suggests, it is almost like being put 'into' the film itself.

Sound with greater frequency range and less noise, colour with higher definition (greater clarity), widescreen, 3D etc can all be combined with production techniques which attempt to emulate human experience. A good example is the opening of *Saving Private Ryan* (US 1998) which was widely praised for its depiction of the D-Day landings. Many veterans suggested that the film recreated the terror and confusion of the real event. For them, and for many younger viewers and listeners, it placed them in the battle scene, experiencing the horror of the moment. Steven Spielberg used hand-held cameras and underwater shots combined with extremely suggestive sound effects to create the effect of carnage in the waves and on the beach. He based the visual images on documentary photographs and shot in such a way that many of the actors were unaware of the camera.

Although this sequence was seen as depicting the violence of war in a 'realistic' way, the film itself remains an example of a transparent Hollywood film. By taking us into the battle, Spielberg is appealing more to our instincts and immediate emotional responses than to our intellectual consideration of 'real events'. The camera in a social realist film would remain much more of a detached observer of the battle, analysing the action and using different soldiers' responses to build up an idea of what happened that day.

Documentary film techniques

Our concern here is primarily with fiction films (and sometimes films based on real events) rather than documentary records of actual events. However, the conventions of documentary filming (including 'observational camera framings', hand-held cameras, voice-overs etc.) can also be applied in fiction films and used to support both Hollywood and social realist films.

Exercises

- Select any two films which might be termed 'social realist'. What is the evidence for this claim?

- Take a contemporary Hollywood film that you think is not 'social realist'. What evidence can you present to support your choice?

- All the main British television soap operas (*Coronation Street, Brookside, EastEnders, Emmerdale*) have been described as deriving from 'British social realism'. Select any ONE of these soaps and indicate the extent to which your selected soap may still be categorised in this way and how far it has moved away from realist concerns.

But

Does realism matter anymore?

Critics and filmmakers have argued at length about realism in the cinema, but recent developments have convinced some postmodernist critics that much of the discussion is becoming irrelevant. They argue that:

- Because digital images can be so easily manipulated and reproduced, it is impossible to tell the 'real' from the 'fictional' so the idea of 'authenticity' has gone.

- Many films and television programmes are 'hybrids', openly mixing 'fact' and 'fiction' styles, so calling a film 'realist' is becoming less useful.

This is a viewpoint you might like to consider in relation to recent Hollywood films based on 'true stories', such as *Erin Brockovich, The Insider*, and *Private Ryan*.

Writing in exams – a note to students

Most of the specifications do not expect you to know all the arguments about realism, but you should be careful in your textual analysis if you refer to a particular type of camerawork as 'realist'. Make sure you describe the technique and relate it to a specific form of realism.

References

Graham Fuller (ed) (1998) *Loach on Loach*, London: Faber and Faber

Andrew Higson (1984) 'Space, Place, Spectacle' in *Screen* Vol 25 Nos 4-5, July-October

Catherine Pouzolet (1997) 'The Cinema of Spike Lee: Images of a Mosaic City' in Mark Reid (ed) *Spike Lee's Do the Right Thing*, Cambridge University Press

Roberto Rossellini (1953) 'A Few Words about Neo-Realism' in *Retrospettive*, 4 April, reprinted in David Overby (ed) *A Reader on Neo-Realism*, Talisman Books 1978

UNIT 3

Analysing the typical

Constructing a representation for a film text is a process of translating a set of complex (and sometimes contradictory) ideas about people, places and events into images that can be understood quite quickly by an audience of diverse 'readers'. All communication must deal with the typical at some level – we often use generalisations to get across our ideas.

In this unit we will concentrate on examining the typing of characters in narratives, however other elements of narratives, such as places and historic periods, are also represented through typing, at some level. Countries in Africa may be typified as poverty stricken, the medieval period of history may be typified as brutal, but the reality is/was often more complex and nuanced.

Characterising people

Human beings are complicated and getting to know someone properly takes a long time. A filmmaker has only a few minutes to introduce characters and enable audiences to get to know them sufficiently well to understand why they act in a particular way. Therefore filmmakers tend to rely on our recognition of types. This constraint is shared by other media, but it is most acute in a fiction film that sets out to tell what might be a complex story in the space of a concentrated ninety minutes or so. A television series or a soap opera will have a longer time with the central characters and more chance to introduce new aspects of their personalities.

Characters in films vs novels

Films are sometimes compared with novels and where a film is an adaptation of a novel, it usually suffers by comparison in the eyes of many critics. They make a distinction between characters in films, who may be 'types' – ie not unique individuals, and characters in novels, who are 'individuated' – fully 'rounded' and believable as unique human beings.

Richard Dyer (1979) suggested the following set of binary oppositions as a starting point in thinking about fictional characters:

Character type	Novelistic character
typical	unique
few traits	multiplicity of traits
immediately identifiable	gradually revealed
pre-given personality	discovered personality
no development within the narrative	develops with narrative
usually a secondary character	usually a central character
indicates society	indicates the individual

However Dyer stresses that the oppositions represent a continuum and that any character in a fiction will be situated somewhere between the two extremes.

Exercise

- Make a list of characters from films and novels that you know well, then place them on a continuum between 'character type' and 'novelistic character'.

Character types are, in fact, used quite often in novels. Some writers emphasise character traits by using names or physical descriptions that immediately suggest a type. In Thackeray's *Vanity Fair*, for example, the cunning heroine is Becky *Sharp*, a cynical old man is Sir Pitt *Crawley* and an honest and unselfish character is Captain *Dobbin* (a dobbin was a workhorse). The idea of a 'vanity fair' is taken from John Bunyan's allegory *Pilgrim's Progress* in which 'Christian' seeks the way to the Celestial City in the company of 'Hopeful' and 'Faithful'. The same approach can be used in films: in Hitchcock's *Psycho* – Norman ('Normal'?) Bates is a serial killer who stuffs birds. The fate of his victim Marion *Crane* is reflected in her name (a crane is a wading bird).

Dyer's oppositions shed light on the distinction between 'novels' and 'genre fiction' and between 'genre films' and 'art' or 'authored films', which lay claim to the status of novels. Genre texts use types extensively and sometimes use them to comment on society generally. Art films are more interested in individual characters, spending time 'fleshing out' characterisations. This doesn't mean that the novel/art film is superior to genre texts, simply that they organise representations in different ways.

Types

We can recognise three different categories of type operating across all media texts.

Archetype

Archetype means literally the 'original model'. Archetypes exist throughout the history of the narrative form. From folk tales and legends thousands of years old to modern stories we come across 'heroes' and 'villains', 'earth mother' and 'prodigal son', 'princess' and 'shining knight' etc. The reference is to a character so well established in traditional stories that the type appears to transcend history or a specific culture.

Generic type

Genres tend to offer a means of discussing contemporary society by using a 'stock' set of characters. These characters are understood more by reference to other films in the same genre than by direct reference to the 'real world'. Each new genre film adds to the repertoire of characters that make up the genre.

Generic types are easy to identify in those genres which have a distinct setting like the gangster film. For example, gangster films from the 1930s to the modern period contain similar generic types in all the films. The power-hungry young man who wants to become the 'boss', the women he becomes involved with (often honest but blinded by love), the white haired mother 'from the old country', the boyhood friend who has become the police officer – these generic types have served as the basis for many similar films.

However, their position in the narrative has changed and the characteristics of the type have evolved. For example, the limited world view and lack of self-control of the earliest gang leader, 'Rico' (Edward G. Robinson) in *Little Caesar* (US 1930) can be compared with the educated and worldly wise Michael Corleone (Al Pacino) in *Godfather 2* (US 1974). The gangsters of the late 1950s had become an integral part of society with more sophisticated business dealings and links to corrupt politicians and police chiefs. The *Godfather* series represents a 'genre re-working' and, because it is a series, there is more time available to explore the characters. Michael Corleone is arguably a more 'rounded' character, but we still learn about him within the framework of our ideas about the generic type of the gang leader.

Genre knowledge plays an important role in the construction of characters as is shown, for example, in *Donnie Brasco* (US 1997). This film tells the story of an FBI agent (Johnny Depp) who infiltrates a Mafia gang after getting an introduction by a veteran Mafia 'soldier' (Al Pacino). The story develops into a 'hybrid' of a gangster film and a 'male melodrama' with our interest in the close friendship, almost that of father and son, between Pacino and Depp. Script writer Paul Attanasio argues that this was possible because he didn't need to fill the script with gangland action – the audience already knew that. The generic typing of Lefty (Pacino) allowed the audience to quickly move on to the relationship with Donnie (Depp).

> **A note to students**
>
> When you are carrying out a textual analysis of any film, it will be helpful if you try to tease out any genre references at the beginning of your work. If you can identify a genre, you may well find that some of the characters are traceable back to 'generic types'.

Stereotype

'Stereotypes' are composite images that represent people and ideas in society by emphasising certain common features. They were developed by social scientists to group people for research projects. New stereotypes are created and recognised all the time. Stereotypes depend on a shared cultural knowledge and to this extent some part of the stereotypical image must 'ring true' for most people.

Compared to generic types, stereotypes are more accessible. As they rely on shared cultural knowledge, readers can readily make sense of them. Popular television (soaps, sitcoms etc) and popular journalism make extensive use of stereotypes. Instantly recognisable people and situations allow the widest access to a story. But this accessibility is both a strength and a weakness. Stereotypes emerge and develop through the repetition in images of features like dress, speech, behaviour etc. Unfortunately, once a character or situation has been introduced in a stereotypical way, it can be difficult to fill in the details and make the image unique. The stereotype refers to assumptions that may already exist in readers' heads, potentially blocking a more considered understanding of the character.

Stereotypes can be very powerful images that embody strong emotional responses. As stereotypes develop, we often respond to them with a sense of identity or alienation – an 'us' and 'them' situation perhaps. The stereotypes that are most discussed are those in which typing as 'them' is clearest. Such images are seen as 'negative' – ie they quickly evoke a person or group seen as 'anti-social' or 'not like us'. People typed in this way are justifiably angry and attempt to challenge the process. This struggle over representation is based on a power relationship where the weaker groups in society can be typed in negative ways.

A few years ago, the Guardian newspaper, hoping to attract 'discerning' readers, ran what quickly became a celebrated television advertising campaign. The advertisement showed a smartly dressed man walking down the street. He is suddenly pushed violently by a youth, identifiable then as the stereotype of the 'street mugger'. As the audience awaits the inevitable snatch of wallet etc, a heavy object crashes to the pavement. The youth has saved the man's life. The inference is clear: the Guardian is a newspaper for those who know that it is wrong to jump to conclusions based simply on stereotypes. Tessa Perkins (1979) went beyond this position and suggested that rejecting stereotypes as always 'bad' is not helpful. She challenged certain myths about stereotypes:

• they are not always 'wrong' in content;

• they do not refer only to 'minority' or 'oppressed' groups;

• they are not necessarily 'simple';

• they are not rigid and can change.

If you remember these four points, you will be able to give stereotypes the consideration they deserve.

Exercise

Types in soap operas

Soap operas provide good material for exploring typing. They often pursue 'universal' stories about families and communities that produce 'archetypal characters' and they must always be accessible to the 'casual viewer' so they also use stereotypes. In addition, the generic characteristics of soap operas influence typing (soaps traditionally feature strong female characters, often as central figures in a 'communal' location like the pub).

• Take your favourite soap and profile some of the leading characters in terms of archetypes or generic types.

• Compare your selected soap with either another soap you know less well or an episode from several years previously (you might find one on cable television).

• How are stereotypes used in your examples?

If you watch a soap over a long period you may notice that when new characters are introduced they are likely to be stereotypical, but the long running time means that they gradually become more 'individualised' (eg the Battersby family in Coronation Street).

Who are the bad guys?

We can also explore the use of stereotypes in action and crime films, for example, by looking at the portrayal of the 'villains'.

Exercise

• Make a list of ten action-adventure or crime films that you have seen. Identify what characteristics the villains in them have in common and what nationalities they represent.

In the last ten years Hollywood has created two villain 'types'. One is usually played by British actors (Alan Rickman in *Die Hard*, both Brian Cox and Anthony Hopkins as 'Hannibal' Lecter) and is typed as 'clever', 'evil' and 'sophisticated'. The other is almost invariably 'Middle Eastern' and is typed as 'devious', 'fanatical', 'cruel' etc. Both of these stereotypes are based on a sense of being 'un-American' or 'other'. The typing of Europeans is not particularly damaging to us and has been part of Hollywood's relationship with Europe since the 1920s. But the typing of Arab culture as 'other' is more disturbing, in that Hollywood is conforming to a government ideology that sees Middle Eastern countries (except Israel) as a potential threat to American power.

These stereotypes work by contrasting the 'honest', 'straightforward' and 'morally upright' American hero with the British/Arab villain. It is a simple power relationship in which the power of the dominant (American) type comes from being the opposite of the British/Arab type. (A neat inversion of this process comes in *Three Kings* (US 1999) in which an American soldier, played by Mark Wahlberg, is being tortured by an Iraqi officer played by Saïd Taghmouai. The Iraqi calmly informs the American that he learned his interrogation techniques from the Americans.)

Exercise – Deconstructing types

• Take any recent Hollywood film that you have seen and try to distinguish the use of archetypes, generic types and stereotypes in relation to two of the central characters.

• Analyse to what extent the same character is archetypal, generic and stereotypical – and to what extent the star image also comes into play.

Representation and challenging stereotypes

One of the main reasons that representation has become a major issue, both within the everyday discussion of the media and in academic film and media studies, is the understanding that audiences are conscious of being 'misrepresented' or not represented at all. For example, in a rapidly ageing population (the proportion of people over 60 is rising), some people argue that there are too few 'representatives' of the whole range of older people in UK society. They suggest that the few characters that do appear, like Victor Meldrew of *One Foot in the Grave*, are easily construed as stereotypes, because they are repeated at the expense of more varied representations.

We tend to notice representations of our own age group or cultural group only when they are clearly 'wrong' (I don't behave like that!) or missing. If we agree with the representation, then we are quite happy. The lack of older people on television is often seen as the fault of the relatively young group of 40 year-olds who commission and schedule television programmes.

However, it is difficult to challenge negative stereotyping effectively. It is not simply a matter of replacing a 'negative' type with a 'positive' one. Under pressure from various African-American Civil Rights groups, Hollywood began to address the representation of black characters and the casting of black actors in the 1970s. They discovered that changing isolated characters in a story led to charges of 'tokenism' (ie the 'token' black police officer in a station house). Black actors wanted to play the full range of parts – they had been the 'victim' or the 'villain', they didn't want now to be only the saintly hero. Hollywood has not solved the problem completely but, as far as African-American representations are concerned, there has been a gradual improvement in the range of roles and representations since the 1970s. To some extent, 'Third World' villains (Hispanic as well as Arab) have replaced African-Americans as representatives of dangerous 'other' cultures.

There is a 'double whammy' in that anyone from a cultural group which is not widely represented in the media must first fight very hard to have a voice at all. But when they do get the chance to 'speak' through the media, there is an expectation that they must speak for everyone else in that cultural group. This has been a particular problem for Black and Asian British performers and writers, such as the quartet behind the television series *Goodness Gracious Me*. The series has been successful, largely by creating comedy that parodies stereotypes of 'Britishness' and 'Indianness', reversing representations to great effect. But now that they have been successful, will the high profile of the performers mean that they are trapped within a particular role? Are they 'representative' of British Asians because their show is the only one of its kind? Will they be criticised if they make a future programme that isn't about the same subject or which appears to criticise other British Asians?

Summary

The difference between types and 'fully-rounded characters' is a matter of degree. All characters, at first, will appear as a type: the kind of person that is being represented. Some characters will develop as a little more detail is added to the first impression, but they remain 'typed' in some way. Major characters are more likely to be gradually 'filled in' with the development of a truly complex character. In less 'deep' films, the main characters may be developed through 'twists' or reversals – a clash of contradictory traits designed to shock or amuse the audience, such as a scruffy character turning out to be wealthy, or a studious, thoughtful character turning out to be brutal and thuggish.

A note about stars

Part of our easy identification of certain types is tied up with our knowledge of stars and their individual 'star image'. Stars, as distinct from 'star actors', are often associated with a specific role which serves to 'type' them over a range of new roles. For example, when Clint Eastwood finally became a star as 'The Man With No Name' in the 1960s, the persona of the outsider was important in the subsequent success of the *Dirty Harry* series of cop films and was then satirised in the *Every Which Way* comedies in the 1980s.

References

Richard Dyer (1979) *The Dumb Blonde Stereotype*, bfi

Tessa Perkins (1979) 'Rethinking Stereotypes' in *Ideology and Cultural Production*, eds Barrett et al, Croom Helm

UNIT 4

Whose voice?

If we accept that all representations are 'constructions', then we also want to know who is responsible for the construction, because it might make a difference to how we perceive and understand the film. We want to know who is speaking through the images we see on the screen, and to what extent the film represents who it appears to represent. For example, are films about working class people actually written and directed by them? Or is someone else responsible for the script etc, and does this matter?

Identifying the 'voice' of a film is complex because filmmaking is a collaborative enterprise and many people may have an influence on how a particular representation is constructed. This means that to a large extent it will be the shared outlooks of the filmmakers rather than the ideas of one or two people that will be important. Even so, the organisation of the process of filmmaking will confer power on a small group of individuals as the decision-makers in each film. The producer, the creative team (director, scriptwriter, cinematographer, editor, etc) and the stars are generally the people who have the most influence over how characters are represented in film. In this unit we explore what this means in terms of who is really 'speaking' – whose viewpoint is actually being represented.

Film Production

Producers

At the top of the pyramid in film production are the producers. They may not be as well known as the directors, but it is their decision as to whether the production goes ahead and, to a certain extent, how and when it is completed. They have influence over the key decisions:

- They choose the subject of the film and will often decide the approach they wish the director to take, given the target audience they identify.

- They raise the money for the film (ie they are responsible for the studio's money) – they are concerned that the shoot will be completed within budget and that the film will be successful with its audience.

- They will probably have the final say in terms of editing the film and re-cutting it if preview audiences suggest that this is necessary.

The creative team

Although the producer may make the initial decisions about subject and approach, the fine control over the representations of people and ideas in the film is ultimately the responsibility of the 'creative team': the director, writer, cinematographer, editors, designers, musical director, etc.

Representing who?

The influence of Hollywood

A major pressure on most producers and their creative teams is Hollywood – or rather the desire to be a successful part of the highly profitable industry that Hollywood represents. Some producers work directly for the studios, while many others are now 'independents', running small companies, and putting together 'packages' to be financed by the Hollywood studios. Most successful producers and directors are white middle-class males living in Los Angeles. Though some are undoubtedly 'liberal' or 'progressive' in the kinds of films that they would like to make, Hollywood as a whole tends to be 'conservative' in its approach. In fact, because its central objective is to sell films, filmmakers in Hollywood necessarily pay less attention to the range of people represented or how they are portrayed.

Hollywood wants to sell films both nationally and internationally and this requires films that entertain without being too disturbing or disruptive of social order. Hollywood films usually employ what is seen as a 'happy ending' and this negates the possibility of challenging established representations. In a film like *Runaway Bride* (US 1998), there is no real possibility that the film could end without the Julia Roberts character getting married – even though there are couples in America who live together and never marry and also women who happily remain single. Hollywood is rarely ahead of audience tastes. Producers may tease audiences with what seem like radical stories and new stylistic

approaches, only to pull back at the end and offer a resolution that drags the story back into the mainstream. Two films worth considering in this context are *Three Kings* (1999) and *Traffic* (2001). Both made by 'independent' directors, these films offer stories about, respectively, the Gulf War and the 'war on drugs'. Both films toy with criticisms of American policy and offer innovations in camerawork and editing. It could be argued that *Three Kings* is more consistent in its (limited) critique, while *Traffic*, in the end, conforms to Hollywood's mainstream outlook.

The dominance of Hollywood in the film industry means that most successful and widely distributed films reflect American ideas and values. Hollywood films introduce American culture to international audiences and help sell the American way of life. They are screened everywhere in the world and their success is reflected in the sales of associated American products (soft drinks, fast food, music etc) that are promoted through, for example, 'product placement' – the prominent display in films of American brands like Coca-Cola, Apple, Budweiser etc. Thus, we should not underestimate the strong link between the representation of American culture and the health of the American economy.

Producing outside the mainstream

The only way for most producers outside the mainstream to make films is to raise money independently and to produce on low budgets. However, while they may keep control over representations, they often find it difficult to negotiate distribution deals that allow the films to be widely seen. In American cinema, this has been a major problem for African-American, feminist and politically radical filmmakers. Films such as *Go Fish* (US 1994), *Do the Right Thing* (US 1989), *Mi Vida Loca* (US 1993) have generally found it a much greater struggle to reach a wide audience than films produced for the mainstream.

Gender representation

Most job roles in film production are 'gendered' in some way. Women are most likely to succeed as producers, writers, (film) editors and (costume) designers. In the last decade, there have been some women in top studio jobs (eg Sherry Lansing, Chair of the Paramount Pictures board) and in control of independent production companies (eg Gail Katz, producer of *The Perfect Storm* (US 2000), Christine Vachon, producer of *Go Fish* and *Velvet Goldmine* (GB/US 1998)). Interestingly, the highest profile job – the director – has perhaps attracted more young women into filmmaking than the less prominent, but equally important, role of the cinematographer – perhaps because this requires more technical skills and production experience (access to training has traditionally been more difficult for women). The female film editor is a convention that goes back to the early days of cinema history, when editing (or 'assembly') was seen as an activity with similarities to the production line of machinists in a clothing factory.

> 'When it comes to technical grades there is still an impression that a man will be more reliable. That's one reason I went into production as well as shooting. Now, 80% of the technicians I work with are women and I choose people who are good at their jobs. It's important to look behind you as well as ahead to make sure that there are younger women coming up.
>
> (Pat Holland (The Television Handbook Holland 2000: p78) quoting a personal communication with director/camera person turned producer, Diane Tammes.)

Research Exercise

- Examine to what extent roles in film production are 'gendered'. You can do this by studying the production credits of a selected group of films.

- Watch the end credits of films on television or video or look at the credits listing in any copy of *Sight and Sound*.

- You can also go to the Internet Movie Database (http://uk.imdb.com) and look up individual film titles (use the 'combined details' menu option to show all the crew roles). Films directed by women are sometimes more likely to use female crew members, so you could look at films directed by Karen Bigelow, Marleen Gorris, Jane Campion, Amy Heckerling, Penny Marshall etc.

A useful source of information is the UK 'lead industry body' for the film and broadcast industries, Skillset. On the Skillset website, at http://www.skillset.org, you will find details of the results of the industry census of 2000, showing a breakdown of female and ethnic minority employment across different job roles in the UK film and broadcast industry.

Ethnic representation

Hollywood studios make films with African-American stars and target films towards African-American audiences. But to what extent are the representations carried by these films derived directly from African-American culture? To what extent do they represent the 'voice' of African-American people? Black filmmakers and cultural critics are themselves divided on this issue.

These questions are equally applicable in the UK. After a period in the 1980s when several British Black and Asian filmmakers were able to make low-budget films with public funding, it has become very difficult to fund commercial Black British films:

'The Britain that is being disseminated on cinema screens around the world is steeped in heritage, literary culture and conventional ideas of class relations. It is also overwhelmingly white, in sharp contrast to our workplaces, high streets and bedrooms which tell a very different story. (Alexander 2000)

This has led some black filmmakers in the UK to set up *bfm – black filmmaker magazine* and to build up a base of black talent capable of producing independently and lobbying for funding.

Skin shades

One aspect of cinema that shows up the 'eurocentricity' of cinema is the photography of dark skin tones. For many years most camera and film manufacturers and technical training assumed that the 'normal' skin tone was 'light'. It was difficult to show a dark-skinned actor in such a way as to accurately represent gradations of skin tone – some black actors were literally 'faceless', in comparison with lighter-skinned colleagues, losing their features in shadows or with underexposure. This is an example of a kind of institutional 'mis-representation'. When directors like Spike Lee started out, they worked with black cinematographers, such as Ernest Dickerson who had developed the techniques to present Black actors well (eg Denzel Washington in *Mo' Better Blues* (US 1990)).

Stars

Stars, because they are actually seen on the screen, play a major role in expressing the 'voice' that is being represented. There is a close correlation between the popularity of stars and the range of possible representations. Consider the 'A List' stars at the start of the 21st century: Tom Cruise, Tom Hanks, Mel Gibson, Nicholas Cage, Will Smith, Jim Carrey, Brad Pitt, Julia Roberts etc. These are the stars whose films consistently attract more than $100 million to the North American box office. It is significant that there is only one woman and only one African-American in this list and it remains a fact that:

- African-American men are more likely to find lead roles than African-American women.

- Male stars are still able to find lead roles even when they pass fifty, but this is much more difficult for women.

- There is more pressure on female stars to conform to fashion and conventional ideas of beauty – being 'badly behaved' or 'dressing down' is more likely to hurt a female star than a male star.

Star persona and performance

Fans watch films in a different way to casual cinema-goers. Identification with stars, or more correctly, the 'star image' or 'persona' (ie the 'representation' of the star that exists on the cinema screen and in secondary media such as TV interviews, gossip magazines etc), is an important part of Hollywood and other commercial film industries. Often it is not the fictional character with whom the fan identifies, but the star persona and the performance. It may be more important for many audience members that Mel Gibson dances and waxes his legs in *What Women Want* (US 2001) than that the character does. The film and its narrative may be quickly forgotten, but a new aspect of Gibson's persona is remembered and may influence how his future films are understood and also how audiences think about male stars generally.

It is noticeable that the popularity of certain stars seems to be related to political, cultural and social events. The action stars of the 1980s were Schwarzenegger and Stallone, but now the stars are less muscular and arguably 'prettier' (like Keanu Reeves in *The Matrix* (US 1999)). It is not just that Schwarzenegger is older, but that the star image built around rippling 'pecs', few words and a lack of emotion is no longer in tune with the current idea of an action hero figure. Bruce Willis is a good example of a star whose image has changed to meet different ideas of 'a hero'. In the *Die Hard* series he represented a similar figure to Stallone and Schwarzenegger, but in the last few years he has managed to change his star image to emerge as a more sympathetic character, as in *The Sixth Sense* (US 1999) and *Unbreakable* (US 2000).

Exercise: The 'commutation' test

You can learn a great deal about 'star image' and the ways in which it can be used in a film through a simple exercise in 'commutation' or 'substitution'.

- Take any pairing of stars who usually take on different kinds of roles:

    - Will Smith and Denzel Washington

    - Demi Moore and Gwyneth Paltrow

- Think of a well known role each has taken on, eg Will Smith in *Independence Day* (US 1996), Denzel Washington in *Philadelphia* (US1993).

- What would happen if you swapped the stars. Would they work in their new roles? What wouldn't work? Would we believe in Will Smith as a lawyer? Would Denzel Washington have the lightness and almost comic timing necessary for *Independence Day*?

If the swap is possible, then the star image is not well-defined and is not contributing much towards the representation, but if the swap is impossible – if the fictional character would be changed significantly, then we can argue that the star persona is an integral part of the representation.

References

Karen Alexander (2000) 'Black British Cinema in the 1990s: Going, Going, Gone' in Robert Murphy (ed) *British Cinema in the 90s*, BFI

Patricia Holland (2000) *The Television Handbook* (2nd ed), Routledge

bfm, black filmmaker: www.blackfilmmakermag.com
Editorial Office: Suite 9, 5 Blackhorse Lane, London E17 6DS, Tel 020 8527 9582

UNIT 5

Ideas about audience

If representations are 'constructed', then to be read and understood they must be 'de-constructed' by the viewers – the audience. This process of deconstruction and interpretation is not necessarily conscious and different audiences respond in different ways. For example, a film that is popular with American audiences may flop in Britain, because it doesn't present the world in a way that connects with a British audience. Some films, and the way they represent the world, will be more attractive to female audiences or audiences from particular ethnic groups. In this unit we will explore how audiences interpret representations in film, and how they increasingly influence these representations through their expectations of stars and the types of film they watch.

Individual responses to films

Exercise

- Select a recently released film.

- Compare your own response to it with other responses from:

    - your peer group

    - your teachers' and/or parents' peer groups

    - viewers' comments recorded on web sites such as http://uk.imdb.com or www.amazon.com (Comments with political perspectives can be found on World Socialist Website (http://www.wsws.org) or from gay and lesbian or feminist publications (eg http://glweb.com/lesbianflicks).)

- In noting the responses of others try to assess whether age, ethnicity or gender makes a difference: are there any patterns to the kinds of comments people make about the film? Are there different national or regional responses: do people in America respond differently to people in this country? To what extent is it possible to identify whether a particular point of view or political outlook influences an individual's response to a film?

We all bring to our reading a different set of expectations and experiences of the real world, other films, books, television programmes etc. A film like *American Beauty* (US 1999) that for some audiences is a realistic commentary on a mid-life crisis, may for others be clichéd nonsense, and for others an insight into an experience they haven't had.

Various aspects of an individual's experience may affect his/her reading of a film, such as:

- being male or female

- age

- experience of the culture reflected in the film

- frequency of watching films or going to the cinema

- knowledge about the particular film (background reading, etc)

- political outlook (including the 'personal politics' of race, gender and sexual orientation).

Preferred, negotiated and oppositional readings

Your own reading might follow a 'preferred reading' of the film (what most people think, or how the film is intended to be read). However among any group of people watching a film, there will be a range of responses to the film as a story and a similar range of responses to representations of individuals, places, cultures etc. These two 'user comments' on Julia Roberts' performance in Erin Brockovich from the Internet Movie Database offer an example of how different responses can be to the same film:

Julia Roberts struggles very beautifully, whilst always appearing exactly like a multi-millionairess pretending to be poor and her performance has all the depths of a puddle.

Erin's genuine compassion can only be felt so intensely by the people she interacts with because she

is a woman. Of course the fact that she is not a perfect career woman, in terms of professional attitude and wardrobe style etc…adds another element of reality as she is not THE perfect woman – yet she succeeds in a lovely way and with such support from us: people watching the movie!

A 'preferred reading' is not necessarily correct – there is no 'correct' way to read a film. If your own response to a film is negative, you might develop a 'negotiated reading'. For example, you may initially reject the way a film represents young people, but once you have considered and discussed it you might understand why it works for some (or most) people. Alternatively you may be willing to 'forgive' the representations because the film is enjoyable in other ways. However, if you reject the representations entirely your reading might be 'oppositional' – you would argue that the filmmakers have failed in their representation of young people, the representations are simply not convincing. Most oppositional readings come from film critics who write from a particular point of view or political perspective. However, no considered reading of a film can be based simply on a political or prejudiced reaction – it should be based on evidence from the film itself.

The importance of the audience

An interest in the audience and what individual audience members think is part of a modern approach to audience theory – sometimes referred to as 'reception studies'. Some studies of audience responses to popular films have fallen into the trap of portraying the audience as 'passive' – willing to accept whatever view of the world the filmmaker offers. However, evidence suggests that:

• Audiences actively make connections, and recognise the construction of characters or ideas in a film.

• In order to entertain, filmmakers must find new ways to develop representations to maintain the interest of the audience. Even genre films, reliant on the recognition of familiar characters, must offer new ways of thinking about these characters to keep audience attention.

Audiences tend to 'use' films rather than simply 'consume' them. Individuals watch films for specific and various purposes. Sometimes we just want to be entertained (and how we like to be entertained varies) but at other times we want to find out about something – about fashion, ways of behaving, different cultures, etc. What may seem 'tacky' or inconsequential to one group in the audience may be of supreme importance to others.

For some people film opens up a new world or offers access to a world they aspire to be part of. Some of the gay writing about cinema reveals how important certain representations have been. In the film documentary *The Celluloid Closet*, Harvey Fierstein explains that even the worst kind of camp stereotype was something he welcomed when growing up, because he preferred 'visibility at any cost – I'd rather have negative than nothing'. His own identity was validated and he had someone to identify with.

The impact of new technology on audiences

The advent of video and of the internet has aided the development of film collections and the celebration of individual films and stars. Films remain in print on video because they sell and there is increasing evidence that fans know what they want and are prepared to pay to get it. Films are becoming more like books to be bought and kept, lent and borrowed and watched again. The opportunity to see a film repeatedly presents the possibility of greater audience involvement, in terms of greater familiarity with (and critical appreciation of) the film's narrative and characters, and how these are represented.

The internet is still a relatively new factor in the production of films, but it is becoming apparent that the intense interest in future films has the potential to influence filmmakers. As rumours are circulated about the next film in a 'franchise' (Who is the next Bond villain? In what direction will the X-Men series go? Will Sigourney Weaver really make Alien 5? etc) producers may start to gauge the acceptability of certain developments on the basis of what fans say.

New technology may also change representations in another way in the future. DVDs offer 'outtakes' and deleted scenes or even alternative endings. Would it make a difference if, with a film like *Thelma and Louise*, instead of driving over a cliff rather than surrender to the police, the two women escape over the border to Mexico? If audiences could decide this for themselves, the concept of preferred and negotiated readings would begin to change.

Research Exercise

The best way to explore the ideas in this unit is to carry out your own audience research. The aim of this particular questionnaire is to explore the links between age, gender, and film choice.

• Use one questionnaire for each respondent.

• Approach as wide a range of different audience groups as possible, including your peers.

• Once you have collected the responses, collate and analyse the information. Construct a series of questions to answer that relate how people choose films to their age and gender, such as:

• What is the most important quality in film for people age 15-25?

• What is the most popular genre for this age group?

• What proportion of respondents in each age group use the internet to access information about a film?

• To what extent is there a clear match between gender and genre preference?

• Write up a short report about the conclusions you can draw from this questionnaire.

Questionnaire – Film choices

1. What age group do you belong to:

☐ under 15   ☐ 15-25   ☐ 26-35   ☐ 36-55   ☐ over 55

2. Are you

☐ Male   ☐ Female?

3. Which are the most important qualities of a film for you:

☐ it is exciting

☐ it is realistic

☐ it makes you think about something

☐ it makes you laugh

☐ other: please identify

4. What is the most important feature of the star of a film?

☐ he/she is attractive

☐ you feel that you can identify with him/her in the role

☐ he/she is believable in the role

☐ he/she is the same gender as you

☐ other: please identify

5. Which type of film do you enjoy most?

☐ action-adventure

☐ thriller

☐ horror

☐ comedy

☐ romance

☐ science fiction

☐ other: please identify

6. Which of the following is most important in making a decision about which film to see:

☐ what the film critics say about a film

☐ what friends who have seen the film say about it

☐ what you thought of the last film with the same star

☐ how the trailer and advertising present the film

☐ other: please identify

7. Do you use the internet to find out about films?

☐ Often   ☐ Sometimes   ☐ Occasionally   ☐ Never

8. Do you participate in discussions about films on the internet?

☐ Often   ☐ Sometimes   ☐ Occasionally   ☐ Never

CASE STUDY 1

American Cinema and Social Class: Erin Brockovich and The Insider

Erin Brockovich provides a good starting point for an analysis of representation in American Cinema. In this case study we 'interrogate' the film, asking the five key questions:

- What kind of world does the film construct?

- How does the film deal with types?

- Who is really speaking?

- For whom? How did audiences respond to the film?

- What ideologies does it represent?

We thus hope to discover what kinds of representations are created in the film and how they contribute to our overall understanding of it. Through a comparison with *The Insider* we will focus on representations of social class.

What kind of world does the film construct?

Erin Brockovich is closer to ideals of 'social realism' than most Hollywood films (see Unit 2). The story is based on a series of 'real' events and addresses a 'social issue'. The film begins with a title card confirming the origins of the story and the central character is based on the woman who carried out the investigation (she also appears in the film as a waitress in a diner, taking an order from Julia Roberts). The style of the film is also determinedly realist:

> While it would be a stretch to say that with such scenes [director] Soderbergh approaches something like a Ken Loach film, his character-based naturalism is wonderfully unforced. There's no modish fascination with the bric-a-brac of ordinariness. For once, Middle America isn't played out as a vast fashion shoot and there's none of the misanthropic anthropology of Todd Solondz [director of *Welcome to the Dollhouse* (1995)] or Larry Clarke [director of *Kids* (1995)]. (Roger Wade, 2000)

Wade makes some important points, but they need 'unpicking'.

The director

Steven Soderbergh is not an obvious candidate for making a 'realist' film, following his experiments with editing and manipulation of the image in *Out of Sight* (1998) and *The Limey* (1999), though *The Limey* reflected sequences from Ken Loach's social realist film *Poor Cow* (1967). Soderbergh is currently a hot property in Hollywood – a gifted director who has moved into the mainstream from the 'independent' sector. In *Erin Brockovich* he experiments again by not doing all the things that most contemporary Hollywood films feel obliged to do, so that the impact of the 'real' story shines through.

Mise en scène

The camerawork is purely functional and the editing classically 'invisible', so that there are very few specific images that we remember (apart from those of Erin herself). Instead, we are swept along in the story. As Wade points out, the film avoids emphasising the ordinariness of the lives of the characters with a celebration of 'trash culture' – there is no implied criticism of anybody because of their class position and characters are not made into 'grotesques'.

Acting style

The acting style is 'naturalist' because the actors have been encouraged to simply do what the character would do in a real situation – there is no attempt to 'perform'. Instead, the action is memorable because of its importance in the narrative. Soderbergh is helped by the careful selection of supporting actors, such as the casting of Albert Finney. A British actor with enormous experience (four Oscar nominations), including in social realist films, Finney provides a muted performance to allow the focus to remain on Julia Roberts (although he certainly 'performs' in the final scene).

But if the other characters are presented 'straight', Julia Roberts as Erin gives a 'star performance'. Few other films appear on the surface to depend so much on star appeal. We are intrigued because Erin is a real person. Was she as outrageous in terms of dress and language as Roberts' performance suggests? Yes, according to the other material that comes with the film on DVD. But, even if Erin is a 'realistic' character, there was a risk that Julia Roberts' sheer presence would 'unbalance' the film as a realist enterprise. The success of the film depends on the sensitivity with which the director integrates Erin's story into the film narrative as a whole.

A different world in *The Insider*?

The Insider is also about real events and real people and it also has a 'legal process' underpinning the narrative. Jeffrey Wigand (Russell Crowe) is a tobacco industry executive who 'blows the whistle' on the attempts by the industry to increase smokers' dependence on nicotine.

Exercise

The aim of this exercise is to compare how the 'real' events are presented on screen.

- Take the sequence in *Erin Brockovich* in which Erin is trying to get in touch with Ed after her court appearance because she wants a job.

- Compare this with the sequence in *The Insider* in which Lowell Bergman (Al Pacino) is trying to make his first contact with Jeffrey Wigand (follow it to the end of the meeting in the hotel room).

- Think about the use of film language, in particular consider:
    - lighting
    - camera angles and compositions
    - locations

- What conclusions do you draw about the approach to realism in each sequence?

How does the film deal with types?

The working-class woman

When Julia Roberts appears at the beginning of the film, she is clearly 'typed' as working-class, or at least as 'not conforming to middle-class expectations'. Consider these points:

- her clothing, shoes, hair and make-up;

- her admission in the interview that she had children very early and couldn't go to college;

- the way she smokes outside the interview;

- the beat-up car she drives.

Doherty (2000) suggests:

> ... Susannah Grant [the scriptwriter] works hard to locate Erin amidst the *declasse* clutter of paycheck-to-paycheck single motherhood. Interior decoration by K-Mart, a kitchen of cockroaches and canned goods, and a banged up jalopy measure out the home life of family Brockovich. But if the furnishings are dull and impoverishing, Erin's closet is a vibrant factory outlet for low-couture fashion. With each new entrance, Julia struts down the celluloid catwalk poured into another trashy outfit.

The first appearance is almost a stereotype and the typing is confirmed by her outburst in court (both the anger and lack of self-control and the swearing are indicators of her lack of understanding of middle class mores). From then on, however, as we learn more about Erin, her character is gradually filled out. We begin to recognise that despite her lack of education, she is more than capable of mounting an investigation. We see that she is a caring mother and that she is prepared to work hard to achieve something. She stands up for her dress sense and eventually she is accepted within the law practice.

It is worth considering how much of our understanding of Erin's character derives from Julia Roberts' star image. Roberts is the biggest female star in international cinema, coming into the film after three $100 million box office pictures. She has a 'strong' personality, a famous wide smile and an undeniable charm. Most attention has focused on the clothes she was required to wear in the part. We knew she had long legs but the emphasis on her breasts, squashed and pushed up in tight, low-cut tops, is something of a shock (although the overall effect perhaps recalls her first big role as the hooker turned society girl in *Pretty Woman* (1990)).

Exercise

Consider the following questions:

- How would the same outfit work on another actress who doesn't have Roberts' star power?

- Could anyone else 'carry off' the transition to Erin as investigator hero?

Other 'types'

The representation of Erin needs to be considered next to all the other people in Ed Masry's office and in the community of Hinckley. Apart from Finney, all of the actors have been cast for their 'ordinariness'. It is noticeable that compared to the glamorous law offices seen on American television (eg *Ally McBeal* or *LA Law*) the workers in Ed Masry's practice are varied in age and body shape and are far from a glamour ideal. Finney (once a virile leading man) has become a crumpled and overweight figure who, even in expensive suits, can't be smart. The people of Hinckley generally look as if they belong in a small town. This ordinariness contrasts strongly with the legal 'suits' who represent Pacific Gas & Electric: an example of a stereotype being used to establish the 'enemy'.

George, like Erin, is first introduced as strongly coded, in this case as a laid-back biker, an ex-hippy:

- long hair, beard and bandana;
- bike, tattoos, jewellery, leathers;
- doesn't work full time.

Does the stereotype suggest a dangerous character or one who has simply 'dropped out' of the rat race? The audience's response to George in his initial appearance will depend on their cultural knowledge about this type of character. Later we learn that George is certainly not 'dangerous', but he may indeed be outside the world of paid work. In a narrative sense, it helps that George is so different to Erin in terms of commitment to work, as this allows the possibility of conflict to develop between Erin's work and home environments.

Working class environment

Erin Brockovich's investigation takes her to the Mojave Desert to the north east of Los Angeles in San Bernardino County. Unlike in *The Insider* there is no attempt to emphasise danger through shadows and expressionist lighting. In this case the sunlight is the impoverishing factor, scorching the earth and with the wind reducing the features to miles of sandy scrub and straight freeways. There is little to do in Hinckley and nowhere to go. We assume that Erin herself lives in a suburb of Los Angeles and drives out to the desert (emphasised in the scene when she rings George from her car to help keep awake on the long drive). Erin's own house is modest and utilitarian like thousands of others in the area – it is not the 'white picket fence' suburb of the mid-west, the kind of home represented as ideal small-town America, nor is it the tenement buildings of New York and the eastern cities. It is simply drab uniformity. The subtlety of the representation of the environment is evident in the cinematography that carefully uses sunlight both as a source of blistering heat and as a golden glow when things go right for Erin.

Class in *The Insider*

The world of *The Insider* is determinedly middle class. All the main characters are either in senior management or in the upper reaches of the media or the law. It is possible to make direct comparisons between the homes of Erin and Jeffrey Wigand. His exudes wealth in the form of furnishings, equipment etc. Even when he is forced to 'downsize', his next house has a computer in the basement. When Mrs Wigand cooks she makes pasta with fresh vegetables, not junk food.

Other comparisons reinforce this contrast:

- When Erin and Ed meet, it is over coffee. Wigand and Bergman meet over a Japanese meal, or in luxury hotels. Wigand and Bergman share an intellectual history. Bergman is presented as a famous reporter with a background in 1960s radicalism and around his office are images from the news stories he has covered.

- When Erin's mobile won't work she goes to a payphone – Bergman walks out into the sea from his beach house. Wigand and Bergman exist in a world of phones, faxes and email. Bergman is so well 'connected' that he can conduct conversations with Wigand, the FBI and the Mississippi public prosecutor whilst working on the streets of New Orleans.

- Wigand is seemingly secure in his middle class world and has a long way to fall when things go wrong. The scene when the FBI arrive to investigate the death threats shows up his vulnerability.

Whose 'voice' is in the film?

There are several 'voices' in *Erin Brockovich*, from the real Erin Brokovich's to the voice of the director, and including several contributions from women involved in the production.

Erin Brockovich herself took her story to Carla Santos Shamberg, partner of producer Michael Shamberg. The Shambergs expressed interest, and suggested hiring professional scriptwriter Susannah Grant. The package was developed with Danny DeVito at Jersey Films and offered to Julia Roberts. Only then was Soderbergh offered direction. Soderbergh has shaped the narrative through shooting and editing. He makes a reference to deleted scenes on the DVD, some of which he had to fight to get past the editor, Anne V. Coates, another woman's voice in the creative process. Soderbergh was undoubtedly a good choice and capable of responding sensitively to the script. Nevertheless, the strong presence of women as executive producer, scriptwriter and star is evident in the attention to the important details of a woman's life, particularly in relation to issues of childcare. However, with the power of Julia Roberts' performance she undoubtedly controls the narrative voice in the final instance.

Exercise

- Whose voices are represented in *The Insider*? Make a comparison between *The Insider* and *Erin Brockovich*.

How do audiences respond?

Erin Brockovich was released in the 'dead' box office period in March. With no 'blockbusters' as competition, a strong opening delivered by the 'star power' of Julia Roberts was converted by excellent 'word of mouth' into a surprisingly good North American gross of $125 million – a 'mass' audience.

The box office take implies also that there was more than one audience grouping – perhaps the subject content attracted a 'green' audience. A select group might be attracted by Steven Soderbergh's growing reputation, but the success will be mainly the result of attracting the casual moviegoer.

We can assume a 'preferred reading' of the film – one which the filmmakers probably intended and most of the audience agree to. It recognises Erin Brockovich as an intelligent woman who finds herself in a desperate situation, but is able to rise above her problems and discover her talent. Hard work and dedication allied to humanity enable her to help a community and find some sort of justice for people who have been wronged. This is the reading that earned the film its Oscar nominations and it conforms to the idea of the 'feelgood' movie. But it isn't the only reading.

Exercise

- Look at a range of reviews of *Erin Brockovich* and check the internet for responses posted about *Erin Brockovich*. What alternative readings of the film do viewers offer?

The Insider was less successful commercially and it is worth looking at audience comments on this film as well. Russell Crowe was Oscar nominated as Best Actor for his portrayal of Jeffrey Wigand, but at this stage he was not the star he has become since *Gladiator*. *The Insider* was presented, and generally accepted, as a more 'serious' film, perhaps almost an American 'art' film. Its producers and distributors did not expect it to attract a mass audience and this perhaps meant there was less pressure on director Michael Mann to go for 'feelgood', allowing him to create 'darker' representations.

Exercise

- Summarise at least two alternative readings of *The Insider* from the audience responses recorded on relevant internet websites.

Which ideological positions are represented?

Ideologically, [*Erin Brockovich*] pivots both ways on the American legal system: lawsuits are the only democratic weapon with which to hobble the titans of industry, but the lawyers who wield the writs and take the depositions are scum...

... However environmentally sound the surface politics, Julia Roberts' astonishing star vehicle is propelled by the oldest of fossil fuels. The ecological mindset is nothing if not traditional. PG&E's crime is not a violation of civil law but a sin against nature, a rape of the land. Male, scientific rationality has poisoned the nurturing soil, defiling Mother Nature and deforming her offspring. The tokens of Erin's fecundity ('They're called boobs, Ed.') are the breastplate of an avenging angel, the earthy mother come to banish the despoilers and nurse her children back to health. (Thomas Doherty *Cineaste* 2000)

Doherty gives some good starting points for a more detailed analysis of what is being represented in terms of environmental and gender politics.

Exercise

- Examine some of the underlying issues represented in *Erin Brockovich*. What ideological perspectives does it appear to represent? Consider, for example:
  - What happens to the victims of pollution who do not have access to smart lawyers?
  - Does *Erin Brockovich* really have a happy ending? Erin does well; and the victims get compensation, but they are still likely to die young from debilitating diseases. What perspective is represented by presenting this as a happy ending?
  - Doherty suggests that Erin is an 'archetype' – an 'earth mother' type, under threat by (evil) male scientific rationality – whose perspective does this represent?
  - Make a similar analysis of the ideological perspectives represented in *The Insider*.

References

Thomas Doherty (2000) 'Review of *Erin Brockovich*' in *Cineaste* Vol XXV No. 3

Roger Wade (2000) 'A law unto herself' in *Sight and Sound*, May (The film is reviewed by Andrew O'Hehir in the same issue.)

CASE STUDY 2

Gender representations in Erin Brockovich, Mildred Pierce and The Insider

> Gender differences are culturally formed. They exist on the basis of the biological, but build a huge system of differentiation over and above it. So whereas your sex will determine broadly whether or not you can bear a child, for example (though even this is not a universal truth), gender-based arguments have insisted that because women bear children, therefore they should be the ones to stay at home and bring them up. 'It's only natural' says a whole social system of laws, tax arrangements, childcare and so on. (Branston and Stafford 1999)

The fact that so much of social life is 'gendered' in some way means that we are all under pressure to modify our behaviour according to prevailing views about what is 'natural' or appropriate in being either male or female. Representations of gender issues are a source of debate and conflict because some critics and audiences see the repetition of certain representations in the media as crucial to the perpetuation or potential transformation of traditional ideas.

In this case study we examine how male and female gender identities have been represented in three films. *Erin Brockovich* and *Mildred Pierce* (US 1945) are films about women – narratives so personal that the films are named after the central character. *Erin* was made some fifty years after *Mildred* and we might expect to see a few changes in the depiction of a woman's life over such a long period. By contrast, the story of Jeffrey Wigand in *The Insider* is hidden behind a more mysterious title and explores the consequences for a man when he puts his career at risk.

Exercise

- Discuss what you understand by the following new stereotypes:

    - 'ladette'

    - 'new man'

    - 'man in a mid-life crisis'

    - 'modern career woman'.

- Select one of the above and search for representations associated with the type in advertisements, news stories, television programmes and films.

Changing male and female identities

One of the main aims of the feminist movement during the 1970s was to challenge assumptions about the role of women in society. The political struggle that ensued concerned both the concrete realities of women's lives – equal pay, abortion rights, discrimination at work etc – and the representations in the media that reinforced traditional views about the 'woman's place in the home'. Films like *Mildred Pierce* were studied as part of this process.

Representations are, to a certain extent, the product of unequal power relationships. Any change in the status of women in society has an impact on the status of men. Many traditional societies that have been defined as patriarchies (ie 'governed by men') produce representations that place women in a subservient position. When patriarchy is challenged and the power relationship changes, men's status is diminished, even if this means a 'sharing' of power rather than a reversal of the relationship. Such a diminution of power may cause a reaction from men as well as be reflected in new representations.

During the 1990s period of 'post feminism', social commentators noted several new trends in female and male behaviour. Young women, influenced by the many changes in women's social roles and attitudes that took place in the final quarter of the twentieth century, seem more confident, 'in control' and assertive. Some theorists have referred to this development as 'post feminist' and see it reflected in the emergence of 'ladette' culture – young women expressing a 'laddish' interest in alcohol and men as 'sex objects'. In schools, girls are often more successful than boys in passing exams and they have been the main beneficiaries of many of the changes in employment patterns.

In contrast, men of all ages are said to be now finding life more difficult to the extent that many critics have identified a 'crisis of masculinity'. The expectation that men will be the main breadwinner and 'head of the family' has been eroded, and men have responded in different ways to this change. On the one hand, there is the 'new man' who represents a less aggressive, more sensitive expression of manhood than the traditional 'he-man' or domineering patriarchal figure. Young fathers, for example, are more likely to share in childcare if not housework. On the other hand, 'lad' culture could be seen as a backlash to the 'new order', with young men reasserting a traditional male interest in beer, football and women as 'sex objects'.

Film and society

Exercise

- Referring back to the stereotype you investigated earlier, what kinds of narratives and genres are used in representing the type in films or television programmes you have seen recently?

Film is not a mirror in which changes in society are clearly and directly reflected. Instead, these changes may be reflected subtly, for example, in the way genres gradually change, when films are made which are variations on, or 'inflections' of, existing genres. In the last twenty or thirty years many films have played with and subverted traditional notions of men's and women's roles, from Sigourney Weaver, for example, playing the action hero in the *Alien* films, to Arnold Schwarzenegger playing the role of nursery teacher in *Kindergarten Cop* (US 1990). Sometimes these subverted images emerge as new generic characters, reflecting changing social attitudes about what it means to be a man or a woman.

The woman's picture

Exercise

- Discuss whether *Erin Brockovich* is
  - 'an old-fashioned star vehicle'
  - a woman's picture
  - an investigative thriller.
- What elements does it have of each of these types of film?

The concept of a woman's picture refers back to the 1940s when the studios produced pictures targeted at predominantly female audiences (which during the 1930s and 40s outnumbered male audiences). Stars like Bette Davis, Joan Crawford and Barbara Stanwyck played 'strong' women caught up in romances and crime melodramas. A central feature of these films was often the 'dual life' of the central female character – in the home and 'outside'. The woman's picture might be defined as:

a movie that places at the center of its universe a female who is trying to deal with emotional, social and psychological problems that are specifically connected to the fact that she is a woman. (Basinger, 1993)

The generic elements of the woman's picture could be summarised as:

- a central female figure caught between the demands of home, work and romance
- a female best friend as support, competing male lovers
- a difficult relationship with a daughter
- the heroine is punished for wanting too much

Mildred Pierce is a classic woman's picture and it is useful to compare it with *Erin Brockovich*. Mildred (Joan Crawford) is a suburban housewife with two daughters, the loving Kay and Vida, the 'daughter from hell'. When her husband loses his job and the couple agree to separate, Mildred must look for work. She eventually gets a job as a waitress and learns the business very quickly. A sequence in the early part of the film displays most of the generic features of the woman's picture. At work Mildred meets Ida, a tough-talking career woman who becomes her best friend. At the same time she must fend off the advances of her husband's ex-working partner and deal with the hostility of Vida who is snobbish and can't bear her mother to be 'working with her hands'. We can represent the dramatic conflicts in the narrative like this:

In the 1940s, several films depicted a woman who sought to better herself and to make an independent life as caught in a conflict between these three sets of demands, while her close woman friend typically had only two sets of demands to deal with. The independent woman could not be seen to succeed in having all three – to do so would go against the prevailing ideology that the woman's place was in the home with the children. Inevitably, she was punished in some way at the end of the film. At the end of *Mildred Pierce*, Mildred finds herself being ushered back into her marriage after the terrible deeds (including murder) committed by Vida – Mildred is implicitly guilty of raising Vida badly.

Erin Brockovich and the 'modern woman's picture'

America in the 21st century is very different to America in the middle of the 20th century. Erin does not face such a heart-rending quandary about work and home. She loses her lover, but this does not seem to be a major blow. Erin is strong enough to take it and carry on. The emotional struggle at the centre of *Mildred Pierce* is simply not there in *Erin Brockovich* – home and love/sex seem to have been downplayed in order to allow 'work' to take centre stage. There are moments when it seems that traditional generic narratives might come into play, such as when Erin arrives home from her confrontation the PG&E lawyers, she finds George about to move out. This is the classic tussle between work and love/sex. But George moves out and life goes on. Even though she may be disappointed to lose George as a lover, he returns to look after the children.

The support of other women is usually important in the 'woman's picture'. In *Erin Brockovich*, there is the beginning of a relationship between Erin and the women in the office, but Erin does not have a close female friend as such. Perhaps this is a function of the importance of the investigation, which takes attention away from Erin's personal life. However, at several points in the story events are played out between Erin and other women. For instance, at the end of the film when the audience learns about the success of the legal campaign, it is through a conversation between Erin and the woman who will receive a large compensation payment. This scene is designed to show George what Erin was fighting for and follows the scene in which Erin triumphs over the slick (female) lawyer who Ed has taken on to the team. We might have expected a scene in which Erin hears the announcement of her victory from a judge, but this is not offered. We conclude that Erin's victory as 'her own woman' is what is important.

Erin Brockovich is a 'modern woman's picture' in that it puts a woman's life 'centre stage'. To be a professional, Erin has to organise childcare and her work means that she will sometimes be unable to see her children at all for a few days. Of course, there is no reason why Erin should suffer beyond the usual ups and downs of a working life, but it does pose a problem for the filmmakers. The desire to present Erin as a woman who can succeed and be fulfilled in the world of work seems to take over the narrative. It even subdues the important questions about the activities of PG&E which could have been used to heighten the tension of the film as a legal thriller.

Erin as an investigative thriller

Most legal investigative thrillers are based on the tension generated by a narrative that depends on a serious threat to the investigator if the legal case fails. In *The Insider*, Jeffrey Wigand loses his family and his career in the tobacco industry. In *A Civil Action* (US 1999) the John Travolta character risks his business to pursue a similar civil case about industrial pollution. *Erin Brockovich*, however, subverts this narrative. Ed Masry reaches a point where his business is on the line – but what does Erin risk? While Mildred in the 1940s is 'punished' for her 'desire', Erin, in 2000, seems to triumph in her ambition without ever facing great danger. The only moment of the kind of tension that is usually generated in a legal thriller comes towards the end of the film when Erin is approached by a man when she visits a seedy bar. For a moment, the possibility of a thriller narrative is teasingly set up. But then it turns out that the man is going to give her the evidence she needs. The thriller potential of the original story has been suppressed to highlight Erin as a modern successful woman.

Melodrama in The Insider and Mildred Pierce

Erin Brockovich also ignores the possibilities offered by melodrama. Melodrama is a loose term that has been widely used in theatre and cinema. It does not define a genre and has been used at various times to mean almost completely opposite things. Here we will use it in the revised way that has been promoted by film scholars since the 1970s.

The word means literally 'music' (melos) plus 'drama' and melodrama refers to the display of the characters' emotions expressed through music, lighting, colour, art direction etc – melodrama is about 'excess'. The subject matter is often the family and the relationships between family members. Often families have secrets – things that can't be said – and the repression of these secrets, means that, instead of being spoken, there is an eruption into the mise en scène, which becomes 'excessive'. In *Erin* interpersonal or family tensions rarely come to the foreground, in contrast to the melodramatic intensity of *Mildred Pierce*.

Mildred Pierce is a woman's picture and a classic crime melodrama framed by *film noir*. Mildred's story is told in flashback as she explains to the police what has happened to her when she is questioned about the murder of her second husband. The mise en scène includes the dark shadows and pools of bright light of *film noir* and the 'prison bars' created by the sunlight streaking through the venetian blinds in Mildred's house. In the confrontations between Mildred and Vida, the intensity of the emotions between them is expressed directly in the dialogue. It is also reinforced through Max Steiner's dramatic music which shifts tone within the scene (and which is introduced in the credits as waves wash against the shore) and because of Joan Crawford's performance with its pronounced gestures and looks.

Mildred, as a woman in the 1940s, has plenty to lose and she loses it – punished for being an independent woman, a mother and a lover. Her eldest daughter despises and betrays her, and her other daughter dies after catching pneumonia. Our expectations are for high drama and the film delivers.

Male melodrama

Male melodramas tend to focus on fathers and the crisis they face in respect of 'leading' and 'protecting' their family. While a melodramatic use of expressionist style *mise en scene* in *The Insider* is primarily a function of the thriller genre, the melodramatic elements of a family in crisis are also played out. The fact that the central character of Jeffrey Wigand does not fit the traditional view of the assertive male heightens the tension.

Wigand is about to 'blow the whistle' on 'big tobacco' and they are out to stop him. The effect on his family is devastating. At the start of the film the Wigands are a conventional nuclear family with a high standard of living, dependant on Jeffrey Wigand's salary. When he loses his job, the family begins to 'downsize', but it is the invasion of the family's privacy that really begins to destroy Jeffrey and his family relationships.

Look carefully at the sequence that begins with the email death threat – itself an 'excessive' signal with the mailbox sound followed by a blood red screen and a message in capitals 'WE WILL KILL YOU, WE WILL KILL YOU ALL, SHUT THE FUCK UP!' The sequence also includes:

- the bullet in the mailbox
- Wigand's admission that he has had emotional problems in the past
- his fall as he attempts to stop the FBI taking the computer away.

Wigand effectively 'breaks down' in this sequence and it is at this point that he decides to go ahead with his testimony (arguably an 'emotional' decision, since he is not thinking clearly or dispassionately). In the next scene in the New York hotel before the taping, it becomes apparent that Jeffrey has not told his wife about his decision and she leaves the table in despair. The final shot in this sequence shows her sliding down the wall of the washroom – a clear signal that the marriage is also going down.

Wigand's response to the danger he faces and the disintegration of his family contradicts our view of the traditional 'male' hero. Instead of taking control and being resolute, he suffers almost like the traditional heroine of the woman's picture. He is emotional and liable to lose control. He is not physically able to defend himself or his family and he feels even more vulnerable because once he has lost his professional status (the respect that came with his high-powered job) he has little experience of fighting at street level.

Wigand is, in Russell Crowe's own words on the DVD documentary, 'just an ordinary bloke' who is overwhelmed by consequences of his decision to 'blow the whistle'. The traditional 'hero' figure in *The Insider* is the Al Pacino character, Lowell Bergman, who persuades Wigand to testify and fights tenaciously to put the facts before the public. He is both in control of the situation and entirely sure of himself, acting as an interesting foil to Wigand's character.

Exercise

- Summarise how the characters of Wigand and Bergman portray contrasting representations of men.

- Compare the sequences in *Erin Brockovich* and *The Insider* where the two main protagonists return from their triumphs on the legal front to a home without a partner (Erin returns to find George about to leave, Wigand comes back from testifying in Mississippi to an empty house and a letter).

  - How important is this scene in each film?
  - What evidence is provided about the main characters?
  - How we are asked to understand their feelings and emotions?

Reference

Jeanine Basinger (1993) *A Woman's View: How Hollywood Spoke to Women* 1930-60, Chatto&Windus

Gill Branston and Roy Stafford (1999) *The Media Student's Book*, Chapter 12, Routledge

THREE SHORT STUDIES IN REPRESENTATION

To explore representation in more detail we look here at three very different films.

1   Run Lola Run: Women and action-romance

The film industry tends to assume that men and women favour different genres. Hollywood executives urgently seek responses from exhibitors on the audience composition for new films. Genres associated with male audiences tend to include action-adventure and science fiction, while those associated with female audiences include romance, romantic comedy and melodrama. Recently, the industry has recognised that there is also a significant audience of young women for horror films.

Hollywood has traditionally tried to combine action-adventure and romance to appeal to a wider audience. In recent years, this action-romance genre has evolved in relation to the representation of women: the leading female character has developed from being the victim/princess to taking on the hero role. An early example of this was in the medical thriller *Coma* (US 1978), in which a young female doctor exposes the trade in 'body parts' stolen from patients who have been 'accidentally' allowed to die in surgery. Writing about the film in 1981, Christine Geraghty noted that while it was not unusual for women to initiate action in crime melodramas, it was new for a female character to use her professional knowledge (rather than sexual attraction) to investigate a possible crime and outwit a pursuer. These actions:

> call[s] into question the form of the film and the traditional role of the heroine, at the level not only of content but also of feeling, of experiencing the tensions of a thriller. (Geraghty, 1981)

Since the 1980s, there have been several female investigators/action heroes in high profile Hollywood films.

Research and discussion

- Consider the following female action roles (look them up in a film guide if you don't know about the character):
    - Sigourney Weaver as Ripley in the *Alien* series
    - Jodie Foster and Julianne Moore as Agent Starling in *Silence of the Lambs* and *Hannibal*
    - Linda Hamilton as Sarah Connor in *Terminator 2*
    - Jamie Lee Curtis as Megan Turner in *Blue Steel* and as Laurie Strode in Halloween *H20*
    - Angelina Jolie in *Tomb Raider*
- Which of these roles do you think are most interesting in commenting on the changing experience of women?
- Concentrating on just the representations you know well, to what extent do you think these roles are still male action roles that have been filled by female stars?

Lola rennt – Run Lola Run

Lola rennt (Germany 1998) shows the potential for the action-romance genre to evolve even further to create a new form in which female and male characters are re-imagined. The premise of the film is simple. Lola fails to meet her boyfriend Manni. Distracted, he loses a bag of money belonging to his potentially violent boss, a diamond smuggler. Unless Lola can replace the money in the next 20 minutes, Manni will have to face the consequences. The film then offers three different versions of what happens as Lola runs across Berlin attempting to acquire the money.

Lola and Narrative

The narrative structure of *Lola rennt* comprises a prologue which includes all the characters who will appear in the film, a short sequence establishing the situation, three versions of Lola's 'run' and a short concluding sequence. What becomes apparent is that over the three attempts to complete the run successfully, Lola is learning about herself and the world around her. In the third attempt she finally reaches a point where by sheer force of will (marked by a piercing scream) she appears to stop time itself. This is a film in which the female character is not only central, but also 'in control' of the narrative. At the end of the film, partly because of her actions (and the knock-on effects that they have), Manni turns out to have recovered the money himself. Far from negating Lola's bid to save Manni, this revelation serves only to emphasise that the film is less about finding the money and more about Lola finding herself.

Lola and genre

The ordinariness of Lola and Manni derives from a specific set of generic references, which like many modern films, relate to a range of genres. The race against time to find the money suggests a suspense or *thriller narrative*. The bag of money is possibly a false focus – the thriller aspect seems to revolve around the fate of the bag, yet when Manni recovers it we realise it was not so important. The film also contains elements of the *youth picture* and *family melodrama*. Lola's family is 'dysfunctional'. Her mother is an alcoholic, her father is adulterous and it is suggested that he may not even be her biological father.

A pair of motifs (symbolic images repeated in different forms) perhaps signal the most important genre reference in the film. At root, *Lola rennt* is a *romance*. Lola and Manni are 'ordinary young people' and what is most important to them is their love for each other – this is what Lola discovers at the end of the film. (This reading is confirmed by the director and star who give a detailed commentary on the DVD of the film.)

Exercise

The love motifs in the film are the colour red and references to hearts and heartbeats.

- To expose this 'discourse of romance' note all the uses of red and all the references to hearts and heartbeats.
- Pay special attention to the brief scenes featuring Lola and Manni between the first and second 'runs' and between the second and third 'runs'.
- Does the evidence produced by this search support the reading of the film as a romance?

Lola as a game

After several references to football, Lola's run starts with an animated sequence which resembles the progress of a warrior/hunter in certain kinds of computer game (a reference that is reinforced by the music soundtrack and the rapid pace of the editing). As Lola progresses through the game she 'learns' and, like the characters in 'level' games, she increases her power. In the final run she leaps over the vicious dog at the top of the steps. One possible reading of this 'film as game' is that it establishes Lola as a modern woman – adept at games that have sometimes been seen as largely for boys. It also refers to the female icon of contemporary gaming, Lara Croft. This is a potentially problematic reference as Lola seems neither 'super', nor overtly glamorous – instead, her clothes and behaviour suggest the 'ordinary'.

The idea of the film as game is emphasised by two motifs referring to time which run through the film – the clock face and the image of the spiral. The clock face is circular but two-dimensional, the spiral suggests a third dimension and the idea of being 'sucked in' until you reach the end. The film contains numerous circles, clock faces and spirals (Manni 'phones from outside the 'Spiralle' Night Club, the animated Lola begins her run down a spiral staircase etc). Perhaps the spiral is like life itself – a plunge into a whirl of experience. Learning to exist in the spiral is like learning to live the way you want.

Lola and realism

Lola rennt also provides the clearest possible demonstration of how to use film and video technology to create different 'realisms'. The director has used five different film/video formats:

- For the 'present' when either Lola or Manni is featured, the filmstock is 35mm and colour – the conventional format for a modern feature film.
- When a sequence is shown representing the past, monochrome filmstock is used.
- If neither Manni or Lola is featured in the 'present', video is used.
- 'Snapshots' – a montage of stills is used to show what happens later to some of the minor characters.
- Animation is used for Lola and the croupier in sequences referring specifically to the game element.

Discussion

- Why did the director want to differentiate these aspects of the film narrative?

---

2 Representation in La Haine

La Haine (France 1995)

- uses distinctive camera, sound and editing techniques to represent two very different locations: a housing estate and the city centre;
- has an obvious 'message' – that society is failing in its attempts to understand and respond to the young people in the housing estates outside Paris;

- is a resolutely 'male' film, focusing on a crisis in male identity;
- deals with issues of ethnicity as an aspect of social exclusion.

La Haine is about twenty hours in the lives of Vinz, Saïd and Hubert, three young men from *les banlieues* – the housing estates located about twenty miles from the centre of Paris. On the previous night there has been a riot on the estate in which Abdel, a friend of the three central characters, has been shot. Vinz has stolen a police revolver in the *melée* and has vowed to kill a policeman if Abdel dies. The film covers the events of the next day.

It is rare to find a filmmaker who sets out to use camera, editing and sound in a directly representational way. Mathieu Kassovitz, the director of *La Haine,* decided to use completely different styles to represent the housing estate where his main characters live and the centre of Paris which is like an alien land to the youths.

For the estate, Kassovitz uses stereophonic sound and a tracking camera with long takes and great depth of field, allowing the youths to walk through the estate and to be seen within the environment which is their home. Deep focus means that everything in frame is in sharp focus. Kassovitz claims that this approach represents the sense of community and identity that the youths experience on the estate. For the scenes in Paris, the camera is used more conventionally with shallow focus and more use of cutting than long takes and tracking. The sound is mono, in tune with the relatively 'flat' image. The overall effect is that Paris seems both an alien landscape and one that, through the editing and tighter framings, seems to constrain the youths.

Exercise

- Compare the differences between the two scenes: (1) on the estate where the youths are barbecuing sausages on the roof and (2) in the art gallery in Paris. Look particularly at
    - camera movement, editing and framing.
    - the famous 'switch shot' when the youths first arrive in Paris and pose on a balcony overlooking the city.
- What particular techniques do you notice in each of the scenes and how are they used?

Masculinity

La Haine is not about gender: it is not interested in the young women on the estates or in comparing how men and women react to events. Its subject is the 'emasculated' young men, unemployed and lacking a sense of purpose and direction. Feminist critics have noted the way that the youths use American street culture with its misogynistic language and violence to express themselves. This phenomenon is recognised as a cause for concern across Europe and North America.

Discussion

- Discuss whether the youths are aware of their predicament and what they can do to escape from it.
- None of the youths has a father they can turn to – can Samir, the police officer who 'springs' Saïd from the police station, act as a surrogate father?

Ethnicity

The 'typing' of Saïd, Vinz and Hubert as North African French, Jewish and West African French (*beur, blanc et noir*) is deliberate, but the main concern of the film is not with the issue of ethnicity as such. Instead the trio represent the idea of 'social exclusion'. By selecting different ethnic groups, the film emphasises that what they have in common is oppression by the police.

Delivering a message

La Haine is a film with a distinct message. Metaphors and symbols are used to represent the argument that French society is heading for disaster and that the breakdown in communication between the police and the youths on the estate is a manifestation of the wider problem of a society at war with itself. At the start of the film, a voice tells the story of a man who falls from a skyscraper and as he falls past each floor, says 'So far, so good…', and the same story is repeated twice later in the film. To emphasise the point, the only use of colour in the film comes in the opening shot. While we hear the story of the falling man for the first time, we watch a Molotov cocktail (a lighted petrol-soaked rag in a bottle) which smashes into an image of the world and bursts into flame.

This image of the world turns up again in a second visual metaphor on a poster which announces 'the world is yours'. Saïd 'claims' this image by changing 'yours' to 'ours'. The statement is, of course, ironic. Paris clearly does not belong to the youths – they are excluded in almost every way. In a third scene, one of the youths tries to 'switch off' the lights on the Eiffel Tower by clicking his fingers, but it does not work – 'that only happens in the movies' says another (the lights go off when the youths move away). In this repetition, the word 'society' replaces the word 'man'. These three 'philosophical' asides create a representation of a political argument about the powerlessness of the youths and the fate of society.

The Piano (Australia/France 1992)

- refers to a genre (melodrama) which uses expressionism and symbolism to represent the emotions of the characters;
- combines representations of gender, class and race in a specific context (colonial experience in New Zealand);
- became controversial because audiences (feminists in particular) read the resolution of the narrative in different ways and audience response generally was very strong, either for or against it.

Ada is a single woman with a young daughter living in the 19th century. She has been mute since the birth of her child and only 'speaks' through her piano playing. Her middle class Scottish family arrange her marriage to Stewart, a settler in New Zealand, but when she meets her husband she refuses to consummate the marriage. Instead she begins a relationship with her husband's land agent, Baines – a man who has 'gone native' and integrated himself into Maori culture.

Melodrama

The Piano has all the classic elements of a melodrama. Emotions are severely repressed and this is represented through the clothing and postures of the actors, the music and the depiction of the natural environment through expressionist camerawork (see Bruzzi 1993). A similar kind of emotional intensity and struggle between different desires exists in *The Piano* as it does in *Mildred Pierce*, but in *The Piano* love and sexual desire are complicated by race, class and family. *The Piano* is potentially a modern woman's picture in which the woman suffers but also perhaps gains a form of freedom in the end. As in *Mildred Pierce* the relationship between mother and daughter is important – in *The Piano* Flora 'speaks' for her mother, but also betrays her.

The central image of Ada's piano works as a symbol throughout the film, much as the motifs in *Lola rennt*, but in a much more dramatic fashion. It is almost as if Ada's sense of identity is represented by the physical presence of the piano and the music that she is able to play on it. When she arrives in New Zealand, she refuses to move from the beach unless her piano can accompany her. It is through the piano and her playing that she develops the relationship with Baines and near the end of the film she appears to allow herself to become entangled with the piano when it slides overboard from the boat. The ending of the film is ambiguous: does she live happily ever after – or is this a fantasy that she experiences as she drowns?

Race and class

The three central characters in the film are 'generic types' from the 'colonial melodrama'. One of the main criticisms of the film is the way it uses the stereotype of the child-like, 'innocent' Maori in order to present a more progressive story about a woman's sexual liberation. The stereotype stresses the 'natural' sexuality of the Maori and by extension, Baines. Stewart, by contrast is called 'old dry balls' and is extremely repressed. The Maori are arguably little more than an exotic 'other' – a means by which the Victorian family melodrama can be played out in an environment which acts as a catalyst for the release of Ada's sexual desire. Baines, the agent, is both socially inferior to Stewart and 'tainted' by his adoption of Maori culture. The racial element means that *The Piano* transcends the taboo of the white woman settler and the 'native' man becoming intimate.

Discussion

- How does *The Piano* compare with *Mildred Pierce* and *Erin Brockovich* as a 'woman's picture' and with *Mildred Pierce* and *The Insider* as a melodrama? Which generic elements do the films share and what differences can you find?
- What do you think Ada wants out of life? How do you understand the ending – does she achieve what she wants?

References and further reading

Stella Bruzzi (1997) *Undressing Cinema*, Routledge (other versions of this material appeared in Sight & Sound October 1993, and Women and Film, a Sight & Sound Reader, Scarlet Press 1993. The 1993 S&S issue also includes comments by the film's design team on their approach.)

Vivienne Clark (2001) *The Piano*, York Film Notes

Jill Forbes (2000) 'La Haine' in Jill Forbes and Sarah Street (eds) *European Cinema: an Introduction*, Palgrave

Christine Geraghty (1981) 'Three Women's Films', *Movie* nos 27/28

Roy Stafford (2000) *La Haine*, York Film Notes

Tom Whalen (2000) 'Run, Lola, Run' in *Film Quarterly* vol 53, no 3

Ginette Vincendeau (2000) ' Designs on the banlieue: Mathieu Kassovitzs' La Haine(1995)' in Susan Hayward and Ginette Vincendau (ed) *French Film: Texts and Contexts*, Routledge

Website for *Lola rennt:* http://www.tykwer-online.de (German with an English version)

BIBLIOGRAPHY

* Student textbooks suitable for exploring the theoretical ideas behind key concepts.

Ally Acker (1991) *Reel Women*, Batsford (A history of women filmmakers.)

Karen Alexander (2000) 'Black British Cinema in the 1990s: Going, Going, Gone' in Robert Murphy (ed) *British Cinema in the 90s*, BFI

Donald Bogle (1994, 2nd edition) *Toms, Coons, Mulattoes, Mammies and Bucks: An Interpretative History of Blacks in American Films*, Continuum (A history of the representation of African-Americans in Hollywood.)

Jeanine Basinger (1993) *A Woman's View: How Hollywood Spoke to Women 1930-60*, Chatto&Windus

* Branston and Stafford (1999) *The Media Student's Book* (2nd Edition), Routledge

Stella Bruzzi (1997) *Undressing Cinema*, Routledge (The role of costume in cinema and how it helps construct 'identities'.) Other versions of this material appeared in *Sight & Sound* October 1993, and *Women and Film, a Sight & Sound Reader*, Scarlet Press 1993. The 1993 S&S issue also includes comments by the film's design team on their approach.)

John Casey (2001), Gerald Levin Interview, Guardian 10 March

Vivienne Clark (2001) *The Piano*, York Film Notes

Steve Cohan and Ira Rae Hark (eds) (1993) *Exploring Masculinities in Hollywood Cinema*, Routledge

Thomas Doherty (2000) 'Review of *Erin Brockovich*' in Cineaste Vol XXV No. 3

Richard Dyer (1993) *The Matter of Images: Essays on Representation*, Routledge

Richard Dyer (1985) 'Taking popular television seriously' in Philip Drummond and David Lusted (eds) *Television and Schooling*, BFI

Jill Forbes (2000) 'La Haine' in Jill Forbes and Sarah Street (eds) *European Cinema: an Introduction*, Palgrave

Graham Fuller (ed) (1998) *Loach on Loach*, London: Faber and Faber

Christine Geraghty (1981) 'Three Women's Films', *Movie* nos 27/28

Christine Gledhill (ed.) (1989) *Home is Where the Heart Is*, BFI (A collection of essays on the melodrama and the woman's film.)

Andrew Higson (1984) 'Space, Place, Spectacle' in *Screen* Vol 25 Nos 4-5, July-October

John Hill and Pamela Church Gibson (eds) (1998) *The Oxford Guide to Film Studies*, OUP (see section on 'Film text and context: gender, ideology and identities')

Patricia Holland (2000) *The Television Handbook* (2nd edition), Routledge

bell hooks (1996) *Reel to Real: race, sex and class at the movies*, Routledge

Pat Kirkham and Janet Thumim (eds) (1995) *Me Jane: Masculinity, Movies and Women*, Lawrence and Wishart

* Nick Lacey (1998) *Image and Representation*, Macmillan

Catherine Pouzolet (1997) 'The Cinema of Spike Lee: Images of a Mosaic City' in Mark Reid (ed) *Spike Lee's Do the Right Thing*, Cambridge University Press

Roberto Rossellini (1953) 'A Few Words about Neo-Realism' in *Retrospettive*, 4 April, reprinted in David Overby (ed) *A Reader on Neo-Realism*, Talisman Books 1978

Elaine Shohat and Robert Stam (1994) *Unthinking EuroCentrism: Multiculturalism and the Media*, Routledge

Roy Stafford (2000) *La Haine*, York Film Notes

Yvonne Tasker (1993) *Gender, Genre and the Action Cinema*, Routledge

Yvonne Tasker (1998) *Working Girls: Gender and Sexuality in Popular Cinema*, Routledge

Ginette Vincendeau (2000) ' Designs on the banlieue: Mathieu Kassovitzs' La Haine (1995)' in Susan Hayward and Ginette Vincendeau (ed) *French Film: Texts and Contexts*, Routledge.

Roger Wade (2000) 'A law unto herself' in *Sight and Sound*, May

Tom Whalen (2000) 'Run, Lola, Run' in *Film Quarterly* vol 53, no 3

Filmography

Suggestions for films to study

A Civil Action (US 1999)

American Beauty (US 1999)

Being John Malkovich (US 2000)

The Blair Witch Project (US 1999)

Boyz 'N the Hood (US 1991)

The Celluloid Closet (US 1995)

Clueless (US 1995)

Crossfire (US 1947)

Die Hard (US 1988)

Do The Right Thing (US 1989)

Donnie Brasco (US 1997)

Erin Brockovich (US 2000)

Godfather II (US 1974)

Go Fish (US 1994)

La Haine (France 1995)

The Insider (US 1999)

Kids (US 1995)

Kindergarten Cop (US 1990)

Ladybird, Ladybird (UK 1994)

Little Caesar (US 1930)

Lola rennt (Run Lola Run) (Germany 1998)

The Matrix (US 1999)

Mi Vida Loca (US 1993)

Mildred Pierce (US 1945)

My Name is Joe (UK 1998)

O Brother, Where Art Thou? (US 2000)

The Piano (Australia/France/ New Zealand 1992)

Pleasantville (US 1998)

Psycho (US 1960)

Pulp Fiction (US 1994)

Raining Stones (UK 1993)

Saving Private Ryan (US 1998)

The Sixth Sense (US 1999)

This is Spinal Tap (US 1984)

Tout va bien (France 1972)

Unbreakable (US 2000)

What Women Want (US 2001)

Welcome to the Dollhouse (US 1995)

Action/romance

Crouching Tiger, Hidden Dragon (US/Taiwan/China 2000) (with female action characters)

Youth pictures

Three charming gay romances:

Beautiful Thing (UK 1995) (Working class boys on a London estate, directed by a woman)

Get Real (UK 1998) (Middle class boys in Basingstoke)

Show Me Love (Sweden 1999) (Young women)

These could be compared with each other or with more conventional teen romances in Clueless or Pleasantville.

Gender relationships

Look at male and female relationships in Hitchcock's films (eg *North by Northwest* (US 1959), *Vertigo* (US 1958) and *Psycho* (US 1960)) and at modern films which comment on Hitchcock, such as *L'Appartement* (France 1996)

Ethnicity

Bamboozled (US 2001) is a controversial but fascinating film from Spike Lee that directly challenges the ways in which the history of African-American stereotypes has been discussed in recent years. It includes a compilation of some of the worst excesses in Hollywood and can be profitably studied with reference to Bogle (1994).

Other representations

Wonderland (UK 1999) offers a strikingly unconventional view of London as a place to live and work, utilising 'direct sound', available light and 'real time' shooting. The view of London life it offers could be contrasted with more generic films such as *Face* (UK 1997) (North and East London gangsters) and *Notting Hill* (UK 1999).

ESSAY QUESTIONS

1. What is there to be said for and against stereotyping in the media? Answer with reference to specific titles. (AQA A level)

The following questions have been adapted from specimen and actual examination questions for different specifications.

2. With detailed reference to two characters (one in each film), compare the ways in which social class/status is represented in two films of your choice. (OCR AS)

3. Compare how representations of social class / status are reflected in the themes and subject matter in two films of your choice. (OCR AS)

4. (a) Explain the meaning of TWO of the following terms:

   stereotypical, realism, representations

   (b) A new television soap opera set in a British city will include several parts for ethnic minority actors. Characters will include a dedicated doctor, a struggling student, an harassed single mother and a shopkeeper. Select ONE of these characters and give a brief character profile, explaining how it challenges more traditional representations in other texts you have studied. (WJEC AS)

5. Examine the poster for the film *Aliens* and compare and contrast the representation of the heroine and the use of narrative enigmas created in the poster with the impressions given by the opening sequence of the film. (WJEC A2)

6. Compare how representations of social class / status are reflected in the themes and subject matter of your two chosen films. (OCR AS Media)

7. With detailed reference to your own research findings, discuss the degree to which gender is an important factor in the work of women filmmakers. (OCR A2 Media)

8. Discuss the representations of masculinity in the films you have studied. You may, if you wish, concentrate on a particular age group. (AS Film)

9. Discuss what you find interesting in the representation of the family and/or gender roles in the films you have studied for this topic. (AS Film)

10. Do the films you have studied for this topic construct a very similar representation of national identity or are there differences across your chosen films? (AS Film)

11 Compare the representations of homosexuality and heterosexuality in the films you have studied. What similarities or differences strike you as particularly interesting? (AS Film)

12. Popular mainstream films are often accused of reinforcing dominant values and of lulling audiences into a passive acceptance of these values. From your film studies, do you agree with this? (A2 Film)

APPENDIX

A note on social class in America

Americans' understanding of 'class' is different to most Europeans' understanding. The concept of social class derives from European economic and political theorists of the nineteenth century. They recognised the importance of social background in determining the quality of people's lives and the opportunities available to them.

In Europe, the collection of statistics on occupational background has become the basis for official classification of socio-economic groups. In the UK we have both the Registrar-General's classification (collated on the basis of census data collected every ten years) and the advertising industry's classification (A, B, C1, C2, D, E). The 'working class' in this country (C2, D, E) is officially shrinking and the 'lower middle class' (C1) is expanding as jobs change.

In America, there has not been the same government interest in occupational background and more importance is given to income. There is no official American definition of 'working class', the nearest to a UK-style definition is 'blue collar', which describes manual or factory-based jobs. 'Middle class' roughly equates to 'white collar' or office-based jobs. Social class in America can be defined as 'the prestige of your particular combination of money, occupation and education' (see the website ww2.gasou.edu/cet/psc250/ch8/index/html).

America is the richest country in the world but it also has some of the biggest differences between 'rich' and 'poor' and the differences are widening. Some 35 million people out of a population of around 270 million are officially in poverty. In European terms, the poorest people in America could be considered an 'underclass' because they have little hope of engaging with 'normal' everyday life. There is no 'welfare state' or National Health Service in America – though the poorest people do get 'welfare' and free emergency healthcare. Those in poverty are disproportionately sick or disabled and in single parent families.

In both the UK and the US, social class is something that people 'feel' and sometimes it is at odds with how they might be classified (in the UK) or perceived by others (in both countries). Both societies claim to be 'classless' but this is far from the case and 'class barriers' still exist. In Britain these barriers are most evident in terms of culture and attitudes, but in America, money is possibly more important. In both countries, class status will be indicated through dress and speech and aspects of social behaviour.

Ethnicity has traditionally played a much more important role in American social life than in the UK – America was founded on the basis of large scale immigration from different parts of Europe as well as on a history of slavery and a more recent influx of people from Central America.

A further difference is the importance of 'rural America' in determining attitudes towards work and culture. Large parts of America are still economically dependent on agriculture and 'primary production' (mining, forestry etc), and American culture draws on a more recent historical past that includes experience of 'frontier life'. In Europe, ideas of social class and 'deference' might still refer back to the aristocratic landowner and the 'landless peasant'. In America, the individual pioneer farmer/working cowboy versus the corporate ranching business is a more potent opposition played out many times in Westerns such as *Pat Garrett and Billy the Kid* (1973) or *Heaven's Gate* (1980). The scenes in *Erin Brockovich* shot in Hinkley offer a modern image of 'city slickers' potentially out of place in the country.

tp
publications

bfi